GOD'S WONDERFUL RAILWAY:

PERMANENT WAY

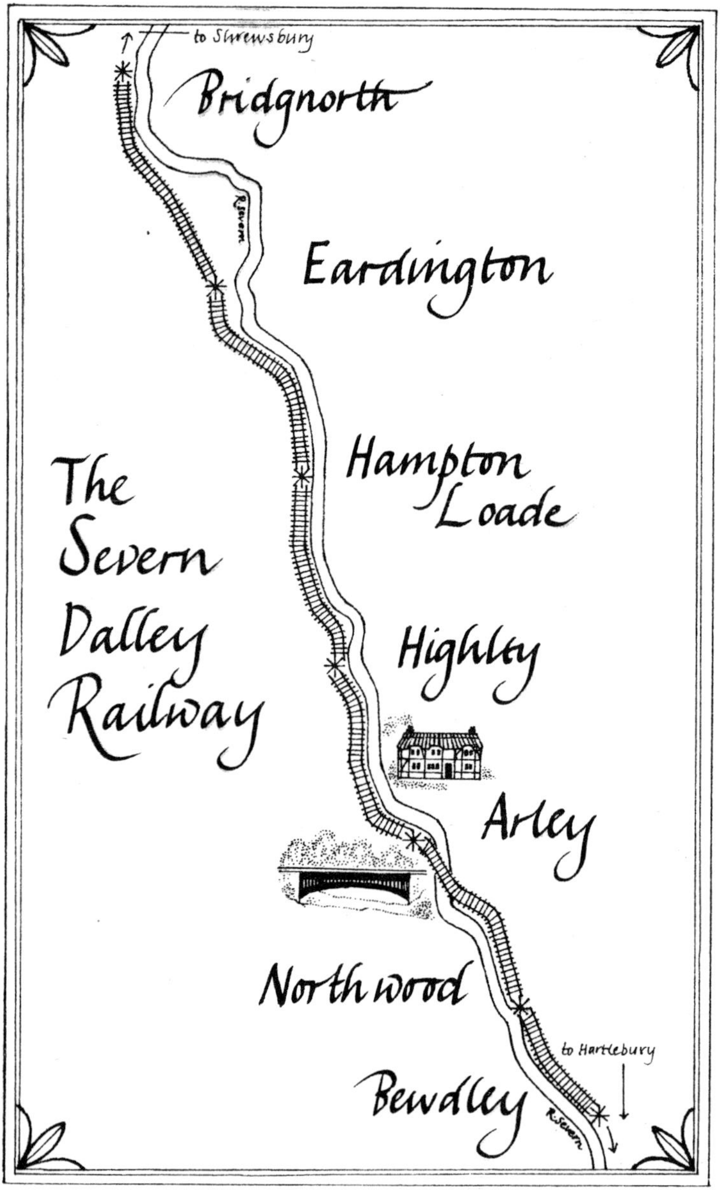

The Severn Valley Railway
to Shrewsbury
Bridgnorth
R. Severn
Eardington
Hampton Loade
Highley
Arley
Northwood
to Hartlebury
Bewdley
R. Severn

GOD'S WONDERFUL RAILWAY:
PERMANENT WAY

Avril Rowlands

BRITISH BROADCASTING CORPORATION

To Christopher;
Alun and Gill Rees,
and my many friends on
The Severn Valley Railway

This story is based on the BBC TV series
GOD'S WONDERFUL RAILWAY first shown in 1980.
It was produced by Paul Stone and
directed by Fiona Cumming. The main characters
who appear in the book were played
as follows: John Grant, Brian Coburn; Robbie,
Gerard Kelly; Martha, Anne Kristen;
Deborah, Anne Burns.

Illustrated by Jo Worth

Published by the
British Broadcasting Corporation
35 Marylebone High Street
London W1M 4AA

ISBN 0 563 17826 4

First published 1980

Printed in England by
Jolly & Barber Ltd, Rugby, Warwickshire

I

"John Grant?"

The big man turned. "Aye sir?"

"The man they call 'The Giant'?"

John Grant nodded. He stood framed in the doorway of the Tommy Shop with a great side of beef carelessly slung over one shoulder.

Mr Bridgman looked him up and down. He saw a big man who towered over everyone, a bearded giant of a man with a mild round face and blue eyes.

"My name's Bridgman. I was told to look out for you. I'm up here recruiting navvies to work on a new line down south. Care to talk about it over a jar of ale?"

Over fresh tankards of ale Mr Bridgman explained further. "Mr Fowler is the Consultant Engineer to the new railway, the Severn Valley Railway as it will be called, and I am on his staff. Mr Fowler said you had a reputation as a good worker and I'm out looking for good workers. He was told that you can out-eat, out-drink, out-swear and out-work any navvy. If that's not an exaggeration you're just the man I need as Head Ganger down at Arley. Interested?"

John was interested. That night he talked it over with his son, Robbie, and early the next morning the two of them set off on the tramp. They were off to build a new railway down south. Off to find a village called Arley in Worcestershire.

In Arley, as indeed in all the towns and villages along the projected route of the new line, feelings had been very mixed about the idea of having a railway at all.

At first there had been much opposition, but by the late 1850s nearly ten thousand miles of railway had already been completed. Many of the people felt that if every other part of the country was either building or planning a railway then the communities along that stretch of the River Severn should not be left without one.

Eventually the arguments were in the main settled; the railway company formed; the necessary Act passed by Parliament; the money more or less found and Mr John Fowler appointed Consultant Engineer-in-Charge. The area had been surveyed, the course of the line finally agreed upon, and nothing was wanting but the men to build it.

Mr Fowler promptly sent some of his staff off to recruit navvies. Railway navvies were the professional railway builders who travelled from job to job wherever there was a new line to be constructed, and Mr Bridgman's hunt took him to the almost completed East Lancashire Railway where he met John Grant.

At about the same time that John and Robbie were making their way south, Mr Cornelius Puddyfoot of Tambour Cottage in Arley died quietly in his sleep. He was a kindly old man whom everybody liked and respected, and his death left his unmarried daughter Martha and his granddaughter Deborah with the cottage and very little else besides. Deborah had been orphaned twelve years ago and was now entirely dependent upon her aunt.

Martha Puddyfoot was a small round lady with a plain round face. She was "not as young as she used to be" as she would say, although she was by no means old, and she was wonderful at what people would call "coping". That meant that she did whatever had to be done and did not waste time daydreaming. Occasionally, very occasionally, she would look in the glass at her plain round face and sigh, but whatever thoughts went through her head at those times she never told anyone.

So when Mr Puddyfoot passed away Martha did not waste time in thinking about what might have been, but concentrated on deciding how best to provide a reasonable living for herself and Deborah. There was one spare bedroom – the best bedroom – and she was thought to be a fair cook. It did not take her long to make up her mind. She would take in lodgers, and who better than some of the people coming to work on the construction of the new railway – the navvies? For by now the navvies were beginning to arrive. In ones, in twos, in groups, in cartloads, they came from all parts of the country. Among them were John and Robbie.

It was late summer and the road glowed and shimmered in the early evening sunshine. John and Robbie had been on the tramp for two weeks and their bright-patterned clothes were thickly coated with dust and grime, but their spirits were high. They looked round as they walked. The country seemed pleasant, and, to their experienced eyes, not too hard for digging, and the pay they had been offered was good, better than the last job.

Late that evening they arrived at the shanty town which had sprung up as always wherever a railway was under construction. They found a shack with two spare bunks, went to the Tommy Shop for provisions and the next day started work.

Two years passed and the work progressed. Two years that, for both John and Robbie, were much the same as other years – hard manual work by day, and drinking, eating and talking by night, interspersed with odd days off and monthly parties on payday. Although the work on this line was hard and fast it was no worse than many they had worked on, for they were both experienced navvies – despite the fact that Robbie was only fifteen.

Robbie had been a railway navvy for some years. In fact he had never known any other life. When he was small he had played around the various shanty towns near his father's work, then he had started to help out, fetching and carrying. Later he had become a truck-hauler – pulling the empty waggons along wooden rails to the workface and removing the full ones to a different part of the works. A few years at that and a pick-axe had been thrust into his hand and he had been told to "get on wi' movin' that dirt an' muck" and he had done little else ever since. It had been hard at first but gradually became easier until now, although he was slightly-built, he could keep pace with the best of them. At least, he could until that dreadful day.

It was hot that day down in the cutting. Robbie was standing, one in a long line of men, hacking and cutting with axe and shovel into the rock. As fast as the truck-haulers brought up empty soil-waggons he and the other navvies filled them. There must have been hundreds of them altogether working there, and hundreds more stretched out along the course of the new railway line.

The sun beat down and every shovelful felt like a dead-weight. The heat made everyone bad-tempered and his father had already stopped one fight between Green-Eye and Baldy.

Robbie came to a stubborn piece of rock and wearily reached for his pick-axe. He was tired, very tired. He lifted his axe and it rose and fell, rose and fell along with hundreds of others, burrowing into the face of the rock, "knocking its legs from under it" as it was called, while the sun burned through his shirt and beat on his skin.

He looked up at his father and his eyes were blinded by the sun. John was tirelessly doing the work of two men and urging everyone else on: "Come on lads – come on there – swing it – harder now!"

Spider, an old navvy with a lined, wrinkled face, stopped to wipe away the sweat. "Stow it Giant," he said, panting for breath, "we're not all built like you."

John turned to him. "Did ye no' hear Mr Bridgman, Spider? They want this line finished in four months."

Green-Eye stopped work and leaned on his shovel. He was a large ill-favoured Irishman who had arrived some weeks back full of big talk about the lines he had worked on. Now he looked scornfully at John. "Ach, rubbish man," he said. "They say that about every railway that's ever been built."

"Right enough," said Spider, "t'ain't our fault work's been held up through the dirt shifting."

There was general agreement with Spider because the work had been uncommonly hard and unrewarding. As soon as the men had dug out a cutting the earth just slipped back in and filled it up again.

"Specially up at Sterns," went on Spider, "killing, that was."

The murmurs and nods of agreement increased. As the men were paid by the amount of earth and rock they dug out, tough digging meant that they earned a great deal less.

"You want your bonus, don't you man?" John retorted.

Spider did not answer. He was a peaceful person and tried to avoid trouble. But Green-Eye stepped forward aggressively. "Who're you threatening, Mr Head Ganger Giant?" he said contemptuously. "Pick someone nearer your own size."

A number of navvies had stopped work by now and were leaning on their tools enjoying the break and the thought of a possible fight. One or two grinned in anticipation. The Giant in a fight was something to see. Fists like sledgehammers he had, or so folks said.

But John ignored Green-Eye and turned to the rest. "Come on you muck-shifters – put your backs into it!" he called. "There's a few more hours' daylight left!"

Green-Eye shrugged, picked up his axe and let fly at a boulder. It split clean in two. Spider looked anxiously from him to the Giant and then quietly went back to work, as did the rest of the navvies, grumbling and disappointed.

That was when it happened. It was Robbie's job that day to lay the dynamite. Once the gang had undermined the rock by burrowing into it from below, it was necessary to blast away the overhang by laying explosive charges.

Robbie pushed the sticks of dynamite into the crevices in a line. He had laid charges like that for years – any number of them. He knew exactly what he was doing – he could have laid them in his sleep. But it was a hot day and he was tired. His head was aching. He fumbled. "Make haste wi' those fuses laddie," called John, "ye're holding up the work!"

"Yes pa," Robbie called back. He hated being told off by his father, especially in front of the others. The sweat poured down his forehead and ran into his eyes. He could hardly see. He heard someone laugh – was it Green-Eye? He started to light the fuses one by one as he had been taught – he shouted a warning and he heard a horn blowing as it always did when explosions were taking place. One fuse would not light and Robbie bent down . . . then a bright, bright light and a sound so loud it was like a pain . . . then blackness . . . then . . . nothing. . . .

Rocks and dust flew in all directions. The men dropped their tools and ran to the spot. John was there first, scrabbling in the dirt, hands cut and bleeding, tearing away at the rocks that covered his son. "Robbie! Oh God, Robbie!" he cried over and over as he fought to lift the large boulder that lay over Robbie's foot, trapping it, crushing it. . . .

2

The offices of Mr John Fowler, Consultant Engineer to the railway company, reflected his growing reputation as one of the foremost railway engineers of the time.

Situated in a quiet, select corner of London, his own office was large – with oak-panelled walls and a good quality carpet – and tasteful, although not lavish, furniture in the heavy Victorian style. It was an impressive room.

On the day Henry Bridgman decided to pay a personal visit to his employer to bring some of the more pressing problems to his attention he found Mr Fowler sitting behind his equally impressive desk. Unfortunately, the ornate carving and highly polished surface of the desk could not properly be admired for it was buried under a mountain of plans, diagrams and papers.

Mr Fowler was a busy man. He was also a rather hard, uncompromising man, and scrupulously fair, except when he was interrupted in the middle of some concentrated work.

He had been interrupted now by his resident engineer.

Henry stood on the other side of the large desk, his hat in his hand, tired and travel-stained and knowing that he had not made a good start with what he wanted to say, but bravely going on nonetheless. ". . . there's bound to be accidents, sir, when the men are asked to work at that speed. It's dangerous and it's skilled work and the men set their own pace. If they hurry they just become careless."

"I am fully aware of that," replied Mr Fowler icily. "I trust you are not trying to tell me my business sir?"

There was an uncomfortable silence. Henry became aware of a clock ticking ponderously and wished it would stop. If only he could start the interview again. He had sat in that dreadful train from Birmingham wedged between a spotty youth who smelt disgusting and scratched and a stout lady who snored with her mouth open and had worked out exactly what he was going to say and the right way to say it. He had even made some notes on crumpled-up pieces of paper, but he could not get them out of his pocket now. He glanced at the only other person in the room, the tall young engineer standing beside Mr Fowler. Benjamin Baker looked back sympathetically. He could have told Henry where he had gone wrong but instead he moved discreetly to the window and engrossed himself in a study of the architecture of the house opposite. But he listened hard. Henry took a deep breath. "No, Mr Fowler," he replied. "All I am saying is that the opening of the railway will have to be delayed if we are not to suffer further, more serious accidents."

"Impossible," said Mr Fowler decisively. "I think, in any event, that you exaggerate. From what you tell me I understand that a navvy laid an explosive charge without due care and injured himself as a result. That does not, to my mind, constitute a row of serious accidents."

"There was also the ganger, Bishop, who was killed excavating Mount Pleasant Tunnel," replied Henry doggedly.

There was another silence. Benjamin Baker would have

loved to turn around to see Mr Fowler's expression, but he continued staring at the house opposite. It was really very ugly he thought, and transferred his attention to a pretty flower-seller in the street below.

"Have you heard the adage about baking a cake, Mr Bridgman?" said Mr Fowler, quietly but cuttingly. "It is not possible to do so without breaking some eggs."

Henry by now was feeling extremely hot and uncomfortable. He wished he had had a drink instead of coming straight from the station. He wished he had freshened up a bit and changed his suit. He wished he had not come. But he was an honest and stubborn man and that remark stung. "With respect, Mr Fowler," he retorted, "we are not talking of eggs. We are talking of men's lives."

"And with equal respect, Mr Bridgman, this absurd sentimentality is misplaced in railway construction. The job of a railway navvy carries with it a certain element of danger. That is why they are so grossly overpaid. That line has to be completed in four months' time – *four months* – otherwise I shall have the Company's shareholders clamouring round my head like a bunch of vultures, to say nothing of the questions in Parliament."

Henry leaned forward earnestly. "But this latest accident has caused problems," he said, "It was my Head Ganger's son who was injured and he feels responsible . . ."

"Well, sack the man and employ a fresh ganger."

"It isn't as easy as that," said Henry, "the man is a key worker."

Mr Fowler turned in his chair. "I'm sorry Baker. I won't keep you."

Benjamin Baker nodded then looked back at the flower-seller. Mentally he ticked off the mistakes Bridgman had made. First was coming in without an appointment looking as though he had just fallen off the overnight train. Second was antagonising Mr Fowler by making demands and not requests. Third . . . but Mr Fowler was speaking again.

"Mr Bridgman, I do understand your anxieties, I am not unsympathetic and I will do my utmost to visit the railway as soon as possible."

This was said in such a dismissive way that Benjamin Baker turned from the window. But Henry stood firm.

"I'm sorry sir, but I really feel . . ."

"I am not in the habit of being dictated to sir," said Mr Fowler, finally losing his temper. "Neither am I involved only in the construction of this particular line. Mr Baker and I were deeply involved in the planning of the course of the Metropolitan Railway when you interrupted us, and in half an hour's time I have to lay the result of those deliberations before its Board of Directors.

"Tomorrow I shall be viewing the progress of the Pimlico Rail Bridge, and at the end of the week I travel to Scotland to discuss with the Duke of Sutherland matters concerning his own railway." He stood up. "I am an engineer Bridgman – I build railways – my responsibilities are to the Companies who contract me. I do not run a benevolent society for injured railway navvies, however worthy a cause that may be. You are paid to sort out those problems. I suggest you do so." He stalked over to the door and held it wide. "Good day to you sir."

Henry walked out slowly. The door shut firmly behind him. There was silence.

"Baker," said Mr Fowler curtly. He was sitting back at his desk once more.

"Sir," said Benjamin Baker and hastily moved to his side.

They resumed work but after a minute Mr Fowler stopped. He got up, went to the window and stared down into the street. Benjamin Baker wondered idly whether the flower-seller was still there.

"I suppose I'd better go and see what's going on down there," said Mr Fowler, "Bridgman obviously can't handle it." He came back into the room and sat down. He thought for a moment. "No," he said slowly, "I won't go just yet, Baker. It doesn't do to underestimate people."

They finished work and left the office. As they were walking downstairs to the street Mr Fowler suddenly dug Baker painfully in the ribs with his cane. "He's got spunk though. Went about it the wrong way, but he stood up to me all right. I liked that. Gave him a rough time too. Cab!" And he ran out of the door and across the street to stop a passing cab.

Benjamin Baker stood and watched him. "Cunning old devil!" he thought. Then he followed Mr Fowler into the street. The flower-seller had gone.

3

The road stretched out like a thin ribbon shimmering in the early evening sunshine. A fine film of dust hanging in the air turned the light into a haze of golden mist. The summer of 1861 had been dry and the ground was parched and bare. Dust was everywhere. It coated the hedgerows and flew up in clouds from the road when the occasional cart trundled by. It was rising now, disturbed by the boy limping painfully along, his rough wooden crutch tightly grasped under one arm, his injured foot trailing dirty bandages in the road.

Robbie Grant had been walking for a long, long time and he was tired, thirsty and in pain.

He stopped to wipe his dirt-streaked hand across his face. It was very still. Even the birds had given up singing. Ahead of him the road twisted on round another bend and the fields stretched endlessly away into a blur of dusty gold. Robbie sighed and slowly walked on.

The sun was a great red ball hanging low in the sky and the shadows were long when Robbie turned off the road and on to a wide, well-beaten path across the fields. It led up to a ridge and Robbie climbed it, pausing frequently to rest. When he reached the top he stopped and looked down.

A narrow cutting had been made clean and straight through the hillside, the gash of red earth showing stark and brilliant against the cornfields lying on either side. The steep slopes of the cutting ended in a strip at the bottom about the width of a narrow road. Along this road, which was not yet smooth and flat but full of boulders and debris, rough and uneven, rails had been laid – temporary rails which came to an abrupt end before a wall of earth and rock.

At this rock-face, down the sides of the slopes and along the bed of the cutting, men were working, hundreds of them. Some were blasting into the rock with explosives of the type Robbie had used; some were digging and shovelling the loosened earth into waggons drawn up on the rails. There were two men working to fill each waggon and they worked in a quiet, concentrated way.

Some men were "making the running". This involved walking precariously up narrow planks laid end to end from the floor of the cutting to the top. Each man pushed a loaded wheelbarrow in front of him straight up the steep sides, aided only by a rope attached to a horse-drawn pulley at the top. Once at the top, he would empty his barrow down the other side of the bank before running back down the plank to repeat the process. There was a steady flow of waggons. Full ones were removed and their contents used further down the line in the construction of embankments and empty ones returned to be filled over again.

The noise was tremendous. Hammering, banging, the grating sound of iron borers, horns blaring out warnings, the muffled thud of explosions – but very little talk. When navvies worked, they concentrated.

Robbie stood at the top and gazed down at the scene. No one looked at him or paid him the slightest attention. He looked along the endless rows of navvies. Then he saw him. He was at the centre of a group of men working at the rock face. A tall man, towering over everyone. "Pa! Pa!" Robbie shouted and started to limp down the slope.

It took a while for John to hear him above the noise, but when he did he looked up. He dropped his spade and started running.

"Robbie!" he cried. "Robbie, lad!"

They met half-way. John looked at him for a moment, taking in his white, drawn face, his crutch, the ugly bandage round his foot. Then he threw his arms round the boy in a great bear-hug. He held him at arm's-length and looked searchingly at him again then looked down as though the sight distressed him. "Ye're no' lookin' well laddie," he said.

Robbie was too tired to speak. He just shook his head slightly.

John turned to the men in the cutting, many of whom had already stopped work to watch what was happening. "All right ye rogues," he called, "there's a half day for you as my laddie's home."

Ironic cheers greeted this and the navvies threw down their tools and started to climb to the top. In a minute Robbie and John were surrounded. Robbie's head swam. Scarecrow, Spider, Baldy, Streaky Joe, Fat-Gut – they were all there, shaking his hand, clapping him on the shoulder, asking how he did.

Green-Eye came over. He stood at the edge of the crowd, grinning slightly, and his voice came clearly through the rest.

"Have to think up a new name for you laddie," he said. "How's about 'Peg-Leg'?" There was a sudden silence. Green-Eye smiled more broadly and went on: "And when do we see you back with us, eh?"

Robbie bit his lip and looked down.

"Ha' done wi' you Green-Eye," called John roughly, pushing his way through the crowd to put his arm protectively round Robbie's shoulders. "Can't you see the lad's dropping?"

Green-Eye laughed and walked off. John watched him go then asked: "Can ye make it to the Tommy? This calls for some ale."

The Tommy Shop was situated midway between the shanty town and the work on the line. Owned by the firm of contractors hired to construct the railway it was little more than a very rough shack with most of the goods crated up in wooden boxes. The shop sold all the things a navvy might need: food, in the form of great sides of beef, bacon, bread, butter and so on; vast kegs of ale, gin, whisky, tobacco, clothes, boots, rope – even blankets and cooking utensils.

None of the goods sold in the Tommy Shop was cheap, but the shop was well patronised by the navvies because it lay close to the works and remained open most hours of the day and night and, most especially, because it gave goods on credit known as "truck". Goods were sold to the navvy and the money deducted from the navvy's next pay.

Robbie and John approached the shop slowly with John taking most of Robbie's weight. "Sit down laddie," said John, gesturing to a wooden bench.

Robbie shook his head. "I'm all right pa," he said, and pushed past John into the shop.

Inside it was dark and the only furniture visible was a rough table and a chair. There was no sign of anyone. John banged his fist down.

"Shorty!" he called. "Come out o'hiding and gie' us some service!"

After a moment a long, thin man with one arm came out from some back recess. "All right, all right," said Shorty crossly, "I'm coming."

He moved nearer and peered at his customers. "Oh," he said in a different voice, "it's you, Giant. What you be wanting?"

"Two tankards of ale an' an ounce of 'baccy," replied John.

Shorty shuffled to the back of the shop and Robbie noticed that he wore soft slippers and not boots. He also noticed that his trousers were held up with a piece of rope like that used in hauling the waggons. But most of all his eyes kept returning to that empty sleeve. It was not pinned up but flapped to and fro as the man walked. Shorty returned. He held two beer mugs in the crook of his arm and the tobacco in his hand. He placed everything down on the table then picked up both mugs.

"You off early then?" he asked as he went over to a barrel.

"Aye," replied John.

"Does Mr Peters know?" said Shorty. He had managed to manipulate the tap on the barrel with his shoulder and was now filling the mugs.

"I'm no' answerable to Mr Peters," John said abruptly.

Shorty looked at him for a moment. "He's your time-keeper 'ent he?" he asked.

"Aye. He is," John replied. "Now will you hurry up, man."

Shorty came back with the full mugs. "This your boy?" he said, nodding towards Robbie.

"Aye." John glanced at Robbie, whose face was white and drawn. He was staring at Shorty as if transfixed.

Shorty put the mugs down and held out his hand. "That'll be fourpence ha'penny. Unless you want it on truck?"

"Aye, I do," said John. "Payday's no' for some time."

Shorty reached for a slate and a piece of chalk. He moistened the chalk with the tip of his tongue and stared at Robbie. "Thought I hadn't seen you around. Had an accident didn't you? Lads was talking."

He started to write laboriously on the slate with much wheezing and sighing and squeaking of the chalk. Then he stopped and again looked at Robbie. "Lost my arm workin' on the line. Never knew that, did you Giant?" he glanced round at John. "Navvyin' up at Woodhead in '48. Lost my footing making a run and went straight down to the bottom with a waggon-load o' muck on top. Lucky to get out alive I suppose."

He went back to the slate. John shifted impatiently. "Will ye come on, man!"

Shorty took his time writing, then hung up the slate. "Followin' year went down with the cholera," he said. "Terrible bad, that was."

John collected the things and went to the door. He called to Robbie, who was still staring at Shorty. Shorty grinned at him.

"There's always work here, youngster," he said. "Could use a spare pair of hands." He laughed and raised the stump of his arm. The sleeve hung down lifelessly. Robbie shivered.

"Come Robbie," called John from the doorway and Robbie turned and stumbled out after him.

Once outside in the fresh air Robbie leant against the wall and closed his eyes. John looked at him anxiously. "You mustn't mind Shorty," he said, "the man's daft in the head."

Robbie did not reply.

"Come, sit down," said John, sitting on the bench.

They sat side by side and drank. An awkward silence had fallen. John spoke first. "How's the foot?"

Robbie shrugged. John went on "You didna' send word you were comin' out o'the Infirmary. I'd have come up to fetch you with a cart. Some of the lads would've come too."

Robbie put his drink down. "It's a long way for you to come," he said. "An' I'm no' a cripple."

Neither spoke for a while. John watched him.

"Ye're no' lookin' well," he said finally. "They cared for you at the Infirmary?"

"Aye," said Robbie, "Well enough."

Robbie leaned his head back against the wall. He was

hating this. He hated talking about his foot, he hated thinking about it. Seeing his mates working away in the cutting had been bad enough, but seeing Shorty shuffling round in his shack was worse, much, much worse. He could see himself in a year's time – no, less – like another Shorty, shuffling round with his hated crutch – "Peg-Leg" to everyone. . . . He shivered again.

"How's the work going?" he asked, looking at his father.

John sat deep in thought, his pipe in one hand, tobacco in the other, making no attempt to fill up. "Very hard," he replied and started to fill his pipe. "They say the line's got to be finished on time even with the land slips – the dirt just slides away under you, and so I told Mr Bridgman."

Robbie was surprised. Mr Bridgman, the engineer living at the site, was not the sort of man to complain to – he was far too important.

"You did?" he said.

"Aye," said John. "After you . . . ." He swallowed hard and did not finish the sentence. "Mr Bridgman's a fair man," he went on, "He said he'd speak with Mr Fowler." He lit his pipe. "Another man was killed two days back."

"Who?" said Robbie.

"Brummagen Bill. He got caught in a rock fall."

He fell silent, puffing at his pipe. Robbie watched him, then leant back and closed his eyes. His head ached as well as his foot and he felt unreal, as though he was living in the middle of a dream.

"Robbie," said John, and Robbie opened his eyes. His father was sitting hunched forwards, staring at the ground, and when he spoke it was slowly, as if it was hard for him. "Robbie – what happened to you – it was my own fault. You rushed that charge because I was pressing you . . . if I hadna' spoken then as I did . . ." he stopped.

"No," said Robbie, "no – you mustn't say that."

"But I *know* it," John said simply.

Neither spoke for a moment.

"I was tired . . . and careless. . . ." said Robbie slowly, "that's all there is to it."

John shook his head and did not look up.

"It was my own fault," Robbie insisted. "Pa, it's *over*."

John looked at him in silence for a long minute, then rose, suddenly. "You're done up," he said. "Can you make it to the village?"

"The village?" Robbie was puzzled.

"Aye," said John. "I'm stayin' at lodgings there. . . . I've moved out of the shanty town."

"No' at the shanty?" said Robbie. "That must be nice. Will your landlord have room for me?"

"Landlady," corrected John. "Aye, oh aye. Miss Martha'll no' turn you away."

Robbie tried to get up but suddenly found that he could not move. His legs would not do what he wanted. John lifted him up easily and carried him away from the Tommy Shop and down to the river. Robbie was dimly aware of being lifted into a boat, "the ferry" he thought, but everything was growing hazy. He started as the boat lurched against the wooden mooring and cried out as his bad foot hit the side. John carried him through the village, up the narrow winding streets until he reached a lane with just one cottage in it.

Tambour Cottage was neat, black and white and thatched. It stood in a small well-tended garden stuffed full of fruit trees, gooseberry bushes, vegetables, chickens, a goat and everything else that was in any way useful. However in one corner was a patch of bright summer flowers which just looked pretty. The walls of the cottage gleamed with fresh whitewash, the fence and gate had been newly painted and the whole place looked loved and cared-for.

John stopped outside the gate, "My lodgings," he said, then opened the gate and went in. But Robbie did not reply. He was unconscious in John's arms.

4

Somebody was doing something to his foot that hurt. Robbie opened his eyes. He was staring straight into a fire and the brightness of the flames made him hastily shut them again. Then his foot was hurt quite badly and Robbie opened his eyes once more and found himself staring at a lady with a round, plain face and kind eyes.

"Am I hurting too much?" she asked anxiously. Robbie was too surprised to answer. He looked round and saw he was in a small parlour. There was not much furniture but everything was spotlessly clean and smelt strongly of bees-wax polish. He was sitting in a large, old oak chair and his bad foot was up on a bench. The lady was kneeling by his side but he could not see what she was doing. There was a table, covered with a white lace cloth and an oil lamp in the centre. Behind the table sat a small dark-haired girl who was staring at him. And there was his father, sitting opposite, anxiously watching both him and the lady.

The lady hurt him very much indeed and he had to

concentrate hard on not crying out. Then suddenly she was standing up and smiling – and it was over.

"There now, it wasn't as bad as all that was it?" she said, but Robbie knew from her expression that she had understood.

He smiled shyly back at her. "No, thank you."

"Deborah'll show you to your bed," she said in a businesslike voice then turned to the girl. "You put a hot brick in it like I said?"

"Yes, aunt." The girl spoke quietly.

"Then you'll be snug and warm," said the lady, "sleep well."

Robbie got up awkwardly. "Goodnight," he said, "and thank you."

"Oh, go on with you," and the lady turned to the pile of dirty bandages lying in a heap on the floor. Robbie looked at John.

"'Night, pa,"

"'Night, son," John replied, smiling slightly at him.

Robbie followed Deborah out of the parlour, up two flights of stairs and into a small attic room. He looked round. It was all white. The walls were white, the curtains white with little yellow flowers, even the bedspread was white.

"It's like – like a palace," he said.

"Oh no it's not," said Deborah. "It's small and poky, I think."

Robbie noticed a shelf with some dolls sitting primly in a row. "This is your room," he said. "I can't take your room."

"It doesn't matter."

"Where'll you sleep? And what about your things?" he gestured to the shelf.

"I'll sleep in aunt's room," said Deborah. "I don't mind – really. And I'll just take . . . Raggedy Ann . . ." and she pounced on one of the dolls, "she'd miss me."

Robbie did not know what to say so he limped over to the

window and looked out. She was being very kind, but he wished that the strange little girl would go away.

"You've been in the Infirmary haven't you?" she said.

"Aye," said Robbie not turning round.

"That's in Worcester, isn't it?"

"It is."

"I've only been there once – to town. I saw the outside of the Infirmary. It looked awfully grim. Is it like that inside?"

"Aye."

Robbie turned round. Deborah was standing in the doorway clutching her doll, watching him curiously.

"You don't say much do you?" she said.

"It's not something I want to talk about," he said shortly.

"Oh," said Deborah, rather crushed. "I'm sorry. Sleep well, Robbie." And she turned and went out. Robbie limped over to the bed and sat down, watched by the row of disapproving dolls.

In the parlour John sat watching Martha as she methodically rolled up the soiled bandages one by one. Watching her deft fingers was somehow soothing, and neither spoke until she had nearly finished. Then he said abruptly, "How bad is it?"

She stopped what she was doing. "I'm no doctor, Mr Grant, and it's a doctor's attention that foot needs."

"But he got that at the Infirmary," John said anxiously.

"Hmm." She resumed tidying up.

"I could ask Doctor Williams in the village to step round," she said.

John did not reply but leaned forward and poked at the brightly burning fire. Martha went on hesitantly: "I – I could add his fee to your bill. . . ."

"No," said John roughly, "I can't be having. . . ."

"You pay your debts, Mr Grant," she said quickly to cover their embarrassment. "Which is more than can be said of some of your navvy friends. Besides, that foot needs attention."

John was silent.

"He's a navvy, like yourself?" asked Martha after a pause.

"Aye. Though I'd not have it so." John spoke so vehemently that Martha was startled. She glanced at him quickly – he was staring into the fire, the poker gripped tightly in his hand. She felt suddenly very sorry for him.

"Well, it'll be some time before he's fit to work again. We'll just have to see what we can do to make the lad comfortable."

She spoke in a flat, rather dry way, but John looked up at her suddenly. She was about to lift the heavy bowl of blood-stained water from the floor. Her apron was dirty and her face flushed. He got up from his chair so quickly that he bumped into her and took the heavy bowl.

"Ye're a kind woman, Martha," he said, "I won't forget it."

And he went out of the room leaving Martha rather flustered.

Much later that night in the small, white, attic room Robbie was having bad dreams. He tossed from side to side, he muttered to himself and once or twice he cried out, "Pa! Pa!" before turning and tossing once again.

Martha heard him as she was going up the stairs to bed. She stood outside his room and listened for a moment, then quietly opened the door and went in, shielding her candle from the draught. Robbie did not wake up. She went over to the bed and put her hand on his forehead. It felt dry and burning. Robbie opened his eyes and stared at her.

"Ssh now, ssh," she said.

"Pa?" whispered Robbie, still half asleep.

"It's late and he's sleeping," said Martha, "do you want me to wake him?"

"No." Robbie moved restlessly.

"You've been having bad dreams. Do you want to tell me?" said Martha, putting the candle down on a table.

"No – I'm all right," said Robbie, but when she picked up the candle and moved to the door he called out: "Please – don't go!"

Martha returned to his bed and sat down. Robbie looked round. "I can't believe it – I can't believe I'm here . . . with pa . . ." and he stopped and closed his eyes for a moment. Martha waited silently. Robbie turned from her and stared at the wall. "I keep having it . . . this dream . . . all the time – in the Infirmary . . . there was just the pain and this dream. . . ." He stopped, then went on in a rush: "Pa's walking away from me – and – and I can't follow . . . because – because I – haven't any legs. . . ." He stopped again. He was trembling and his forehead was wet with sweat.

Martha took his hand. "It's all right now – it's all right. Go back to sleep and I'll stay here with you."

Robbie gripped her hand tightly. "Thank you," he said. After a few minutes his eyes closed and his grip relaxed.

Martha moved away. As she reached the door Robbie spoke drowsily. "Pa said you were kind. . . ." and he fell asleep.

5

It had just begun to get light and the first grey streaks of dawn threw into outline the shacks and huts of the shanty town. Apart from a lonely cat sniffing round a pile of rotting rubbish all was quiet and still.

A figure came out of one of the huts, yawned, blinked, stretched, then disappeared inside again. From another hut a voice shouted out crossly. The cat turned and fled into the shadows.

It grew lighter and men started emerging from the shacks. A low hum of noise began – a clink of metal, the odd muttered word, the stamp of heavy boots – noise swelling gradually louder and louder to a crescendo as the shacks emptied until the paths between the huts were full of jostling, pushing, cursing, talking navvies.

As the sun rose the brightly-coloured mass could be seen, in ones, in twos, in groups, in a steady stream, straggling over the hill and down to the railway. They stood out incongruously against the dark mud and wood of the shanty and the soft misty green of the early morning hills.

No less incongruous were the one or two navvies to be seen hurrying down the village street. Dressed in their white felt hats, their brilliant striped waistcoats and with gaudy kerchiefs tied round their necks they stood out conspicuously from the usual early risers in the village – the farmworkers, the miners on their way to the coal works at Kinlet and the clay workers heading for Shatterford.

One of the navvies hurrying down the village street in the direction of the river was John. Some way behind him, limping badly as he tried to catch up, was Robbie.

"Pa! Pa!" he called. John turned round then stopped.

"Robbie! What are you doing up at this hour?"

"I couldn't sleep," Robbie confessed. "And – I thought – you'd maybe take me on as a truck hauler."

John was shocked. "No Robbie," he said, and turned to go.

"Why?" pleaded Robbie.

"Ye're no' fit for work. And anyway. . . ." John broke off.

"What?"

John did not answer.

"What, pa?" insisted Robbie.

John walked on. "I must be on my way," he said, "I'll miss the ferry."

"It's about my foot isn't it?" said Robbie, limping along besides him. "Isn't it?"

John did not speak.

"What did Miss Martha say to you?" He held on to John's sleeve and looked up at him anxiously.

"She said it's not good. She said we ought to get the doctor to it," said John, reluctantly.

"Doctors!" repeated Robbie scornfully. "Where've we money for them?"

"I'll find it, never you worry."

"No," said Robbie, "I'm not taking money from you."

"Robbie!"

"I'll no' be a burden on you," said Robbie, evenly and decisively.

John did not answer. They reached the riverside and John watched as the ferry was pulled by the swift flowing current of the river into midstream. Then he said slowly, "There's other work besides building railways."

"Running a Tommy Shop like Shorty?" John looked up in surprise at the bitterness in Robbie's voice. Robbie went on, "Pa, I'm scared. Navvyin's the only thing I know. What'll I do if I can't labour? Go to the workhouse?"

"No," said John firmly, "no, ye'll not do that." Then he was silent.

The ferry reached the opposite shore and John watched the people get off, shadowy forms half-hidden by the sun shining on the early morning mists that rose from the river. Faint sounds could be heard: the ferry creaking, a snatch of talk, a horse whinnying. The ferry began to move back across the river.

"It's my own fault," John said. "I should never have brought you up to a navvy's life. You want to settle down somewhere."

"You haven't. . . ." returned Robbie.

"Aye, well . . ." John was silent. "It's too late for me. I couldna' settle now."

Abruptly he strode off to join the group waiting for the returning boat. Robbie watched him go then turned and limped away up the street. He wandered aimlessly round the village not wanting to go back to the cottage just yet. The sun rose high in the sky and it was going to be another hot day. Two ladies came out of a house and stared at him curiously and he had never felt so lonely in his life.

Some hours later Deborah found him on the river bank idly throwing stones into the water.

"Oh, hello – I was looking for you," she said. "Aunt sent me to find you."

Robbie scrambled awkwardly to his feet. "Yes, Miss Deborah?"

Deborah burst out laughing. "Don't call me that! Nobody calls me that – it sounds so funny."

Robbie stood silently, twisting his hat in his hands, wishing she would go away.

"Aunt said that she's asked Doctor Williams to call," Deborah went on. "He'll be along soon, so if you'll come back with me . . ."

"She'd no need," said Robbie stiffly. "My foot's well enough."

"Aunt didn't think so," replied Deborah. "She said they didn't know that they were about at the Infirmary."

Robbie stood unmoving.

"Oh, come on do," urged Deborah taking his arm. "She'll be awfully angry if I go back without you."

Reluctantly he walked off with her. "I'm sure your aunt's kind, but she shouldn't have bothered," he said.

She did not reply and they walked on in silence until they turned into the lane leading to the cottage. "You are a prickly sort of person aren't you?" she said.

Robbie flushed red. "I don't know what you mean," he mumbled. They had reached the garden gate and Robbie struggled to open the gate with one hand while not dropping his crutch with the other. Deborah slapped his hand away and opened it for him.

"I'm only trying to be polite and aunt's only trying to be kind," she said, "and you go all bad-tempered about it." She stood back waiting for him to enter.

"I'm sorry," said Robbie gruffly.

"That's all right."

As they went into the garden she looked at him and suddenly giggled. "You look just like my pet hedgehog when it's got all its spikes out," she said.

"Do I?" said Robbie mystified.

"Yes," said Deborah. "I'll show him to you if you like, then you'll see."

And she smiled at him in such a friendly way that he could not help smiling back, although he was not sure that this was the right thing to do. He had never known any girls before and he found Deborah slightly alarming.

"That's the first time you've smiled," she said, and they went into the cottage.

The Resident Engineer's site office was a small, clean, functional room. Its only furniture comprised a plain desk and one chair. All the walls were covered with plans, diagrams and charts and the small window looked out at a brick wall. Henry Bridgman was standing by the window when John came in.

"You wanted to see me sir," said John.

"Oh yes. Grant, as from tomorrow you'll have to split your butty up into shifts – two sixteen-hour shifts overlapping morning and evening. I've informed the other gangers already. We've to start night working."

There was a moment's silence. "That doesna' make sense Mr Bridgman." Henry did not reply. John continued: "We're workin' as fast as we can. I'll no' press the lads any further."

Henry went to his desk and sat down. "I did speak with Mr Fowler about the various problems we've had. He was . . ." he groped for the right word ". . . most sympathetic, but there is nothing he can do. The opening can't be delayed. And that means working faster I'm afraid."

"I'll no' put another man's life in danger because of it," replied John stubbornly.

Henry felt most uncomfortable as he was entirely in agreement with John but could not say so. It was very difficult giving orders you disagreed with, he thought. He tried another approach.

"Look man, I've been working with navvies for thirteen years – you don't have to tell me about the risks and the dangers. It's not easy to get skilled men right now, so the Company have agreed to increase every man's pay by one shilling a week with extra beef rations until the work is done." Henry paused for a moment. "It'll be a fine achievement – this railway. Something to be proud of."

"And I'll be as proud of it as the next man," retorted John, "but a shillin' a week's no' what it's about."

"Isn't it? I think – in the end – that it is." Henry hated saying it. He looked at John. He liked the man. He liked him very much. "Look, Grant, I did try," he went on. "There is nothing more I can do. If you are not prepared to get the lads to work as required, then I shall have no alternative but to dismiss you and employ another Head Ganger from among your butty – Green-Eye for example."

John smiled in spite of himself. "Ye'll no' get a good man there," he said mildly.

"I am aware of it," said Henry, slightly stiffly. "I don't want to do that because I have a respect for you and the way you work." He stopped and looked up at John. John was standing, solid, immovable, filling the small room with his large presence. Henry went on gently, "And I think the money won't come amiss to you either. Doctor's fees are expensive."

There was a sudden silence and Henry knew that he had won. The knowledge made him feel rather cheap. "I'm sorry," he said and looked down at his desk.

John turned and walked out.

He returned to the cutting in no good mood and started to work furiously. After one glance at his set face the other navvies did their best to avoid him. In a short time the lad who was keeping him supplied with empty waggons to fill could not keep up and John was left standing fuming.

"So there ye are at last Rusty," he said angrily as the boy

staggered up pulling a number of empty waggons behind him. "Am I supposed to be sitting idle while I wait for the setts?"

Rusty muttered an apology and ran off. Green-Eye stopped work.

"Are you after another accident then Giant?" he called, "You after maimin' all the youngsters?"

John turned to him, slowly. "Ye'll take that back, Green-Eye," he said threateningly.

"The hell I will."

The two men eyed each other. John gripped his shovel tightly and took a pace towards him, but was stopped by Spider, who nervously placed himself in John's path. "Och – come on man," said Spider, "tek no notice o' him. The Irish are all mad anyway."

That broke the tension. The navvies surrounding them laughed and John went back to his place.

"All right Spider," he said, then raised his voice. "Ye'll have no breath to laugh with soon lads – we're workin' nights as of tomorrow."

The laughter changed to questions and exclamations. John went on, "There's a shillin' a week in it for each man, an' extra beef. Now let's get on wi' it."

Green-Eye started to speak but Spider nudged him. "I wouldn't cross him Green-Eye. He's a big man."

Green-Eye spat contemptuously and returned to work. Gradually the pace increased and there was no more talk.

Robbie was sitting in the parlour in the big chair he had sat in the previous night when Deborah tiptoed in carrying a large tray. She glanced at him and saw from his expression that he had had a rough time at the doctor's hands. She placed the tray on the table.

"Here's some soup," she said in a whisper.

Robbie started. "What?" he said.

"And some bread rolls. They're fresh," she went on, still in a whisper.

"Why are you whispering?" asked Robbie.

"Aunt said I should be quiet because you're poorly," she said in a normal voice. "Here's some soup and rolls. Aunt thought you'd like them."

"Thank you," said Robbie. He grimaced as he moved his legs to turn to the table. "She's very kind."

"Only to people she likes," said Deborah.

"Well, she can't like me," said Robbie. "She hardly knows me."

"She likes Mr Grant though," said Deborah, putting the soup in front of him.

Robbie looked up at her, surprised. "Pa?" he said.

"Oh yes," went on Deborah, "no other navvy's ever been invited to the parlour of an evening." She nodded at the soup. "Drink it up while it's hot." Robbie obediently picked up the spoon.

"I like him too," said Deborah reflectively. Robbie understood that.

"He's – he's . . ." he hunted for the right word . . . "the *best* there is." He picked up a roll and bit into it. "Oh – this is good," he said, and ate it greedily.

"You're not like other navvies I've met," Deborah said consideringly. "Ones that have stayed here I mean. I don't know any others. Neither's Mr Grant really."

Robbie finished the roll. "I don't know about being different," he said, "I'm not anyway – pa is. I've always wanted to be like him. Folks look up to him – they trust him. He's so brave . . . and strong." He stopped suddenly. "But I'm not like him at all and now – now I'm just a burden . . ."

He pushed away his plate and sat brooding. A hand falling on his shoulder made him jump. Martha had come quietly into the room.

"Deborah," she said, "let Robbie have his meal in peace. Have you finished shelling those peas?"

When Deborah had gone Robbie looked at Martha. "What – what did he say – the doctor?"

Martha sat down. When she spoke it was slowly, picking her words with care. "He said – given time – and treatment – it will get much better."

"How much better?" Robbie demanded. He was watching her with big, fearful eyes.

"He couldn't say," said Martha.

"Will I – will I . . . always be lame?" asked Robbie.

Martha looked at him in her kindly way but did not speak. Then she looked down at her lap. Robbie sat quite, quite still.

6

The next day the fine weather broke and it rained hard. As if to make up for so many dry weeks, it continued to rain, day after day, and it was cold and blustery. The navvies worked knee-deep in mud and swore as much against the wet weather as they had against the dry. The torrential rain brought a section of hillside crashing down on the newly laid permanent track and for over a week every navvy worked round the clock to repair the damage and shore up the hill.

Robbie had to remain indoors resting for much of the time and so he and Deborah were thrown closer together. Gradually he stopped feeling strange and even began to like her. She was younger than he was and looked up to him as though he were an elder brother which he found pleasing but rather odd. Nobody had ever looked up to him before.

Deborah was always asking questions and he began to realise how very little he knew even about things that closely concerned him. One evening she asked how navvies had got their name and he admitted that he did not know. It was

Martha who told them that the name had come from the old canal builders who had been called "Navigators". Robbie felt very stupid then.

But there were things he could tell her. He could tell her about building railways, and he could describe how the navvies went about the work of digging out cuttings, tunnelling, making embankments and laying the track. He also explained to her about engines and tried to describe how they worked, "like enormous kettles on wheels". Deborah just smiled and shook her head and he was amazed to learn that she had never seen an engine.

But what really caught her imagination was the shanty towns, and she was for ever asking Robbie what they were like and how he had liked living in them.

"Haven't you seen the one near here?" he said idly one day. "It's only just outside the village."

"Aunt won't let me," she said regretfully.

"Well, that's probably just as well," he said, having second thoughts.

"Why – what's the matter with it?" she demanded.

"Nothing," he said.

"Will you take me to see it then?" she asked swiftly.

"No – not without your aunt's permission," he replied firmly. But Deborah could be very persuasive and very single-minded and a few days later, quite without knowing how, Robbie found himself walking with Deborah over the fields in the direction of the shanty.

They reached the first straggling huts and after passing through roughly marked off areas containing cows, horses and pigs, they soon found themselves in a maze of narrow paths bordered on either side by shacks and huts of all description.

Deborah looked eagerly about her. Some of the huts were almost like poorer versions of the cottages in the village – neatly constructed buildings of wood and stone with well-made roofs. One even had some vegetables growing in a patch of earth fenced off from the path, but that was the exception. Most of the huts had been thrown together with whatever materials lay to hand; old wooden sleepers, rusty iron, turf, stones, old tattered blankets: anything in fact that would afford some protection from the weather.

They walked on. Chickens, cats and dogs got in their way and the recent rain had turned the earth to thick mud which made walking difficult. There were few people about as most of the navvies were at work, but those there were stared curiously at them. Children, ragged and barefoot, peeped out from the huts and a group started to follow them but were soon sent off by Robbie.

They passed open spaces where huge fires had been built. Some were alight and steaming cauldrons swayed on wooden poles above the flames. Everywhere lay great heaps of things – tools, waggons, ropes – big untidy piles lying where they had been thrown.

Deborah stopped outside a hut and peered in. Near the entrance hung great sides of beef and Deborah could dimly make out a rough table, a couple of benches and a great mass of ropes, boots and clothes hanging down from the roof. Behind the table, stretching back into the gloom were what looked like large wooden shelves with piles of blankets on them. They were set against the walls in rows from floor to roof and Deborah realised that they must be beds.

The place smelt. It smelt of stale sweat, dirty clothes, unwashed bodies and above all an indistinguishable aroma which rose from a pot suspended over an open fire.

Someone hurried into the hut, pushing past her. It was a woman. She was dressed in rags and Deborah could not tell how old she was because although her face was lined and grey, her hair was jet black. Once inside the woman turned and smiled and Deborah saw with a slight shock that she had no teeth.

"I should never have brought you here," said Robbie as Deborah backed away from the hut.

Deborah turned to him. "Who is that woman?" she asked.

"Cross-eyed Mary," said Robbie.

Deborah laughed. "What a funny name," she said. "Does she live there?"

"Aye. She's married to Baldy. Come on, it's not right you being here." He hurried her along the paths, away from the shanty and out into the open fields.

"What were all those beds for?" Deborah asked after a pause.

"Navvies," Robbie replied. "She takes in lodgers. Pa and I stayed there a while."

"That's where you lived?"

"Aye."

"Just in that one room?"

"Aye."

"How many of you?" Deborah persisted.

Robbie shrugged uncomfortably. "I don't know. Sometimes – fourteen or so – sometimes maybe twenty– it depends."

Deborah was silent for a while.

"And you've lived in places like that *all* your life?" she said suddenly, and Robbie nodded. "Who brought you up?"

"Pa."

"What about your mother?"

"She's dead," he replied briefly and reluctantly.

"So's mine," said Deborah, "*and* my father."

They did not speak again until they had reached the village. Robbie followed Deborah and found himself being led into the churchyard. She went straight to a grave.

"There," she said, gesturing to the lettering on the headstone, "you see, they died twelve years ago."

Robbie turned away. "I can't read," he said awkwardly.

"Oh . . ." Deborah was surprised. "I didn't . . . they died

in a cholera epidemic."

"I'm sorry," said Robbie.

"You needn't be," she said, "I don't remember them at all. My mother was aunt's sister." She turned and walked off and Robbie followed. When they were out of the churchyard she looked at him. "Did your mother die a long time ago too?" she asked.

"Yes."

"What did she die of?" asked Deborah, interested. She was pleased to find something they could share, even if it was only that neither of them had a mother.

"I don't know. I don't know anything about her." Robbie was acutely uncomfortable.

"Nothing at all?"

"No. Pa's never told me."

"Haven't you asked?"

"No." Robbie would have liked to change the subject but he did not know how.

"Why?" Deborah insisted.

Robbie could not look at her. He spoke mumblingly to the ground. "Well . . . navvies aren't like other folk," he began haltingly. "They have – different ways of doing things – and sometimes – sometimes there's not a wedding in church . . . if there's not a church nearby . . . there's only a navvy wedding and. . . ." he trailed off miserably.

"You are – Christians – aren't you?" Deborah asked, fascinated and a bit shocked.

"Oh yes," Robbie assured her, "well I am – and pa is. . . ."

"But you mean – your mother and Mr Grant might not have been married?"

"Oh no," said Robbie, with an assurance he did not feel. "No. I don't know. It's different for us – like I said . . . and I don't like to ask. I can't ask pa those sort of things. . . ."

There were things, he thought, you could not ask because nobody did. Nobody questioned where they came from because all too often they could never find the answer. Robbie had wondered in the past but he had never asked. He had wondered about the women that lived on the shanty, cooking the meals, looking after him and other children in a rough kind of way, drinking, sometimes fighting, going from one man to another . . . he had wondered – but he could never ask his father. Somewhere deep inside he was too afraid. Of course, it was the same for everyone, he thought. Nobody asked another man about his past because when you were a navvy, provided you could do the work, eat two pounds of beef and drink a gallon of beer a day, you were accepted. Why, navvies even had different names from the ones they were christened with – if, indeed, they had ever been christened at all.

But he could not explain any of that to Deborah – she just would not, could not, understand. It was a world away from her clean, white, attic bedroom and the bright polished parlour that smelt of beeswax.

As they had walked round the shanty town, he imagined seeing it through her eyes, and for the first time in his life he was ashamed of it. He was both ashamed and unsettled – if he felt like that, how could he ever go back?

"And you've only ever lived with navvies?" Deborah's voice broke in on his thoughts.

Robbie nodded.

"And travelled about?" she went on.

"Aye," he said, "all over the country."

Deborah sighed. "It's awfully exciting," she said enviously.

Robbie turned to her, surprised. He'd got it all wrong, he thought. She did not disapprove at all. He grinned wryly. "I don't know that I'd call the shanty exciting," he said, "neither's the work. It's hard, dirty and dangerous." But she was not to be convinced, and they went home.

He swore to himself that he would not let himself be

persuaded into anything like that again, but a few days later when he had gone into the village with Deborah to do some shopping, she thought of something else.

"I've never seen a train, you know," she said.

"Aye, you told me."

"Everybody else has," she went on, "aunt has travelled in one and she said it was very fast and very noisy."

"It is," he said, not wanting to be drawn.

"And it was big and blew out steam like a dragon," she continued.

"I don't know about dragons," he said, confused.

"There must be some about," she said, "not too far away . . .?"

"Dragons?" he said, now totally confused.

"No, trains, silly."

"There's only works trains," he said unwillingly, "and you'd no' like them. They're only small."

"I would like them," she said, "they wouldn't be small to me. *Please* Robbie . . .?"

"You must ask your aunt," said Robbie, feeling trapped.

"She never said I *couldn't* see one," said Deborah, "she just never said I *could*. She's always too busy to take me."

"I don't know where there is one. It might be miles from here."

"We could take aunt's pony and trap," Deborah replied cheerfully. "You wait here, and I'll see about it."

She thrust the basket into his hand and ran off. A few minutes later she had returned in a small trap and Robbie reluctantly climbed up. They were soon bowling down the lane out of the village.

"It's a bit frightening, you know," said Robbie, still trying to discourage her, "the first time you see it."

"Why?" asked Deborah.

Robbie did not know how to explain. "Well, you'll see," he said lamely.

"I'm not scared of anything," said Deborah proudly.

Robbie grinned. "Are ye not then?" he said.

But when they reached a section of new track she fell silent. Robbie climbed out and went over to a group of navvies who were working there. He came back to her.

"Come on," he said, "get down. The lads said there'll be one along in a minute and you'll see better from the track-side."

Deborah climbed down the cutting. She was beginning to feel slightly nervous, and jumped when she heard a distant rumbling noise. "What's that?" she said, alarmed.

"That's her coming. Stand still," said Robbie, for she had jumped again at the sound of a whistle. Deborah stood still and looked obediently up the track. Surely there was smoke rising?

"There's a fire, Robbie," she said, tugging his sleeve.

He laughed. "There's a fire in the engine! I told you about it."

Deborah did not want to know about it any more. She wished she had never asked anything about engines, trains or railways. Nearer and nearer it came until in a cloud of smoke and steam it was upon them. The ground shook, or so it seemed to her. It was like a monster – it was like a great fiery dragon – it breathed hot air – Deborah did not wish to see any more.

Once it had passed Robbie looked round. "Deborah?" he called, "Deborah, where are you?"

She emerged shame-faced from the bush into which she had dived. It was a bramble-bush and Robbie helped get her out while she sucked her pricked fingers. "I thought you weren't scared of anything!" he said.

"It's so big – and all that smoke," she said. "It looked as if it was from the devil."

Robbie just laughed. His face was alight and he sounded excited. He seemed a different person from the Robbie she knew. "That's only a small engine!" he scoffed. "You should see the ones on the main London lines. Twice the size at least, they are, and they can travel really fast. Why, you can get from Birmingham to London in under three hours now!"

As both places seemed as far away as the moon to Deborah, the information did not mean very much, but his excitement was infectious.

"I've only been on small engines, mind, but even that's tremendous," he went on. "The engine-driver on the works train would sometimes take me up and let me stoke the fire for him . . ." He stopped, and like a shutter the light went out of his face. ". . . but that was some time ago," he said and even his voice was different. "She's coming back," he said. "You watch, this time."

Deborah stood still and watched as the small engine came down the line towards them. It had a tall funnel, she noticed, where the smoke came from, and a place at the back where two men stood. One was bending down, putting something into a red, glowing hole with a shovel. Then the engine was past, and the train of empty waggons clanked and banged along behind. When it was gone Deborah let out a big sigh.

"We'd best get back," said Robbie sounding grim and curt. "What time's your aunt expect you?"

They started walking to the trap. "Well, she doesn't really," said Deborah, "you see – she doesn't know I've gone."

Robbie stopped. "You never told her?" he said.

"She wasn't there to ask," Deborah replied simply.

Robbie hurried off.

"Robbie! Wait!" cried Deborah, hurrying after him.

Once in the trap, Robbie took the reins. "Your aunt will be furious," he said, as they drove along at a spanking pace.

"Yes, I expect she will," agreed Deborah.

"And she'll be quite right," went on Robbie remorselessly. "Suppose she needed the trap?"

"I never thought of that," she said in a small voice.

"You don't think, do you?"

Deborah sat silent for a moment. Then she said: "Robbie?"

"What?"

"If we had one of your steam engines we'd get home ever so quickly. You could drive it and I . . ."

She had only said it idly, to make him laugh and to take the bleak look from his face, but his reaction frightened her.

"Don't talk stupid," he said, more harshly than she had ever heard him speak before.

"I'm sorry," she said in a whisper. He did not reply. "I said I'm sorry," she repeated a bit louder.

When Robbie spoke it was in a tight voice and he was not looking at her, but straight at the road in front of him. "I wanted to be a driver. I thought maybe when there were no more railways to be built, I could get a job driving engines. It's something I've always wanted . . ." his mouth was set in a thin, hard line.

"Well, why can't you?" Deborah asked.

"You've got to be fit, that's why," he replied shortly. "An' I'm no' fit any more."

And he whipped the pony on harder.

7

From then on Robbie retreated behind a grim, silent wall which Deborah could not penetrate. She showed him her pet hedgehog and laughed at the resemblance she said she could see between them. She took him round her patch of garden and pointed out the various late summer flowers. She even offered to lend him Raggedy Ann, but she did so fearfully, fully expecting a scornful rebuff. Robbie was not scornful, but nothing she tried could take away the bleak look from his mouth or make his eyes light up as they had that day by the trackside.

His foot steadily improved under the doctor's treatment, but progress was slow and he still needed his crutch to help him walk. He was restless and irritable. He felt stifled in the cottage and would escape from it as often as he could. He would spend hours each evening in the alehouse, sometimes with his father, but more often alone, not speaking, not drinking much, just listening to the navvies talk. They talked a language he knew, and he felt at home there.

When any stranger appeared, usually a navvy passing through the area, Robbie would be the first to go over to him and he would sit listening avidly to what the man had to say about where he had come from and where he was bound.

Once he asked his father what they would do when the line was finished, but John, usually the first to know about fresh work to be had, the first to give a strange navvy a "tramping bob" the money for food and ale – and the first to ply him with questions, was strangely silent.

"There's not so much work around as there was," he said at last, reluctantly. "There won't be many new lines to build soon, I reckon, unless ye've a mind to travel overseas. I heard Mr Brassey was wantin' men to travel to India to build railways for the Empire over there."

"India," repeated Robbie, half-scared, half-excited by the prospect.

"Aye," said John, giving Robbie a sideways glance. "But I've no' a mind to go there myself. England's overseas enough for me." And he fell silent and would not be drawn into further discussion.

Robbie also spent more time near the construction watching the progress of the line. He would limp along, to watch the embankments grow every day as waggon after waggon upturned its contents on the tops and down the sides of the banks.

He watched drains laid, culverts made over streams, road and rail bridges erected, and he would walk along the finished track, eyeing it professionally. Generally, though, he could be found sitting wedged between two rocks watching his father's butty at work in the cutting – but he was careful not to let himself be seen.

He was there one day almost asleep, watching his father's shovel fly rhythmically up and down. His father stopped work and Robbie was dimly aware of him calling out angrily for more waggons. Another navvy answered and Robbie sat bolt upright, fully awake. Green-Eye's words came clearly over to him.

"Sure it's your own boy'll be doin' that soon enough. Don't be too hard on Rusty now!"

Robbie was on his feet, groping for his crutch. He heard his father reply, "Robbie'll no' be drawin' the sets. He's no' a labourer. He's a navvy."

Robbie stopped still, his hands unconsciously clenching and unclenching. Green-Eye sneered back, "Was a navvy, don't you mean? He's no more'n a cripple now – and who's to blame for that, Mr Chief Ganger Giant?"

Robbie limped forwards and saw his father put down his shovel and carefully begin to take off his jacket.

"Ye go too far, Green-Eye," he said.

"Pa!" Robbie called. "Pa!"

Green-Eye turned. He saw Robbie and started to smile. "Well, well, an' if it isn't the little cripple lad himself," he said.

Robbie moved towards him.

"Keep out o' the way Robbie," his father ordered. His jacket was off and he was rolling up the sleeves of his shirt. The other navvies had stopped work and were crowding round.

"Yes – out o' the way cripple," said Green-Eye, pushing Robbie to one side. "This is between men."

"All right Green-Eye," said John Grant quietly, "all right."

Robbie looked from him back to Green-Eye. His father had his fists clenched and stood watching Green-Eye impassively, waiting for him to make a move. Green-Eye took a step . . .

"I'm as good a man as you, Green-Eye," Robbie called, and to his disgust his voice was trembling, "Aye, and as good a navvy. . . ."

"Robbie!" John called sharply.

Robbie swung round on him. "And I fight my own battles, pa." He looked round at the watching men. "I'll show you."

He looked round the cutting. Nearby stood a heavily-laden barrow. He limped over to it and picked up the handles, dropping his crutch as he did so. With a great effort he stood upright, balancing the weight against his body. There was absolute silence. Taking one slow step at a time he limped with the barrow over to the start of a run. The barrow wobbled precariously as he went and small rocks and stones fell from it. He looked up. The planks, laid end to end, seemed to rise almost vertically up the steep sides of the cutting and were slippery with mud and rain. A rope ran from the pulley at the top down the planks and ended at his feet. Robbie's fingers shook as he attached the rope first to the barrow and then round his waist. He manhandled the barrow onto the first plank and looked up again. Small against the skyline stood a man silently watching him, holding on to a horse.

"Pull!" he yelled, and his voice was firm.

"No, Robbie!" cried John. The man at the top hesitated.

Green-Eye was watching Robbie closely. He looked up and called, "Do what the lad says. Pull!" and he was no longer sneering.

Robbie looked up again. Beside the man a small figure had appeared – Deborah. She called down to him, "Robbie, no!" He gave her a slight, a very slight smile, then nodded to the man at the top. The man started leading the horse away from the run and the rope tightened over the pulley. The slack was taken up along the length of the planks and the barrow jerked in his hands.

Robbie slipped and he heard a sharp intake of breath behind him. He steadied the barrow and put his bad foot firmly down on the plank.

Two horsemen could now be seen on the skyline. They

stopped and looked down. They saw the silent crowd of watching navvies and Robbie at the foot of the run. Henry Bridgman rode forward. "What the devil . . .?" he began, but Mr Fowler, the other horseman, stopped him. "Wait," he said. They checked their horses and watched.

A shooting stab of pain made Robbie close his eyes for a second. The rope pulled taut. John watched him closely. With agonising slowness Robbie walked up the steep planks. There was no sound from the cutting. Everyone there knew how dangerous it was. Absolute steadiness was needed to make the running and only the strongest men attempted it. If Robbie slipped or faltered in any way he would have to try and throw the heavy barrow to one side and himself to the other if he was not to be showered with a hundredweight of rubble and muck.

John bit his lip. If that happened – or if he fell down the slope with his bad leg – and he was only a lad and out of trim. . . . He watched the slight figure with painful intensity.

But Robbie was not thinking of what might happen if he fell. He needed every ounce of concentration to put one foot firmly in front of the other, to ignore the stabs of acute pain, to keep himself upright and the barrow straight. The horse at the top pulled the rope smoothly and steadily through the pulley and steadily and smoothly Robbie inched his way up the muddy planks. Near to the top he briefly looked up. He fleetingly saw Deborah, her hands pressed to her mouth, and he saw the two men on horseback. His concentration broken, he slipped on some mud. He gasped, and a sigh went up from the navvies below. He could feel himself sliding backwards, and with a last great effort he pushed the barrow up and over the top of the plank then threw himself to one side. Friendly hands rushed to help and prevent him from rolling down to the bottom. A great cheer resounded round the cutting. John raced up the slope and was beside him almost as fast as Deborah.

"I'm all right," gasped Robbie, pushing away the helping hands.

"No laddie," said John firmly, lifting him up into his arms. He straightened and caught a glimpse of Green-Eye turning and walking away, then he carried Robbie off and Deborah followed.

"A brave lad," said Mr Fowler thoughtfully as he watched them go. Then he turned to Henry. "Well Mr Bridgman?"

"I'll just send the men back to work, sir, and we can proceed to the bridge," replied Henry.

"High time sir, high time," replied Mr Fowler.

8

Robbie had done no real harm to his foot, but he had to rest for several days. He did not mind that. He did not mind the doctor tut-tutting over him or Deborah constantly running in and out with an endless supply of food, flowers, brightly-coloured picture books and anything else she could think of to keep him from boredom. He even endured patiently the efficient care from Martha and the blunt scold from his father. He was at peace – he had proved himself. Only one thing puzzled him about the incident and at the first opportunity he tackled his father.

"Why does Green-Eye seem to hate us so, pa?" he asked one evening.

John had helped him down to the alehouse and they were sitting outside, facing into the early evening sun, tankards of ale in front of them. John did not speak for a moment. "I wouldna' call it 'hate' laddie," he said thoughtfully after a moment. "'Envy' perhaps, 'dislike', but no' 'hate'. An' it's not aimed at you."

"Well why?" Robbie persisted.

"I don't know." John thought for a moment, then shrugged. "He'd like to be Chief Ganger I suppose. He doesna' like playin' second string . . . an' I stopped him takin' a knife to his woman that night – you remember, you were there. An' then of course there was the trouble over Miss Martha."

"Miss Martha?" Robbie was surprised. "What was that?"

"Chance," said John, "just chance." He lit his pipe and puffed away at it.

"It was payday. You were sick in the Infirmary an' what wi' one thing an' another I'd made up my mind to get roaring drunk. An' I did. It was quite a randy that – fightin' going on all over the village with the farm lads from the estate – drinkin'. It took three days before we had all the butty back at work and at least another week before we were workin' to a fair pace." He paused. "Well, I must have looked a fair sight by evenin' what wi' the drink an' the fight with Green-Eye."

"Fight?" said Robbie. "What about?"

John shrugged. "Oh, this an' that – I don't remember now. That man'd pick a quarrel with his own shadow." He laughed. "So would I, given the amount of ale I'd drunk. After it was over I wandered round a bit. I was in the village and I suppose I was tryin' to find the ferry but I was walking in the wrong direction. Well, I ended up in the lane leading to the cottage and there, believe it or not, was Green-Eye. He was standin' on the doorstep tryin' to push his way in past Miss Martha."

He stopped to take a drink, then wiped his beard absently. "I can see it now, that great hulkin' oaf of an Irishman with a string o' curses rollin' off his tongue. He was lookin' a sight too – every bit as bad as me if not worse. An' there was Martha – all five foot nothing of her – standin' in the doorway, a big rollin' pin in her hand, keepin' him out. Deborah was there too, red-faced and crying, but not

Martha," he smiled slightly, "no, not Martha. She was cool as you please. 'I don't lodge drunkards in my house', she said. That set Green-Eye off worse than ever and he started to push and shove his way past her."

"What did you do?" asked Robbie, enthralled.

"I went into the garden, up the path and raised my hat – or what was left of it from the batterin' it had during the fight, an' then I said, 'Anything I can do for you ma'am?' She gave me a look that put me about the same level as Green-Eye, and said: 'I'd be obliged if you would remove your friend'. 'Delighted ma'am,' I said, 'but he's no' a friend of mine.' I threw Green-Eye out into the road and walked back. 'He won't be no trouble to you again,' I said, 'I'll see to it.'"

John stared down into his mug, a smile playing round the corners of his mouth. "She looked up at me – a straight look – and said, quite calmly, 'I'm obliged, sir'. Just that. No faintin' in my arms or going off into hysterics or whatever most women do. Just, 'I'm obliged, sir'.

"Well, I turned to go, but she called me back. 'When you're clean and sober I've a room to let here if you've a mind.' I did have a mind. The next evenin' I was back, sober, cleaned-up, dressed in my best and wi' my hat – which I'd cleaned up too – in my hand. She met me at the door just the same as the night before, but without the rolling pin – an' that was that."

As they walked slowly back to the cottage, Robbie kept glancing sideways at John. There was something in the way his father had talked and the way he had looked that was different. But whatever it was had gone as John joked and chatted with the couple of navvies who went with them down to the ferry. Anyway, Robbie could not ask. He shrugged his shoulders and concentrated on climbing unaided into the boat.

Martha had also noticed a difference. John spent more time

in the cottage in the evenings and less at the alehouse, and did odd jobs for her too. They started when he found her angrily chasing the goat round the garden late one afternoon. The goat had uprooted the stake it was tethered to and was enjoying the unexpected freedom.

"Just look at my cabbages!" Martha had said, half-laughing, half-despairing, as she tried to catch the string with the stake on the end which the goat trailed behind her. "That's the fourth time Jemima's done that. Come here, you bad goat!"

John helped catch the goat and then had driven a fresh stake firmly into the ground. After that he had mended a door, repaired the thatch after a storm, and become indispensable in all sorts of ways.

Martha began to rely on him in a way she had never done with anyone else. She knew it and she would shake herself angrily. "Martha Puddyfoot," she would say to herself, "this won't do. He's a navvy. When this line's finished he'll be off like the rest of them and never a thought for you or anyone else. You know the sort of reputation navvies have. Besides, you've managed quite well up to now without any of that sort of nonsense, and you're far too old now. And furthermore," she would go on to herself, "you're short, plain and well past thirty. No one in their right mind would look twice at you."

But sometimes in the evening when they sat companionably in front of the fire – sometimes talking, sometimes silent – John smoking his pipe and Martha sewing, she would feel so comfortable with him and he seemed to understand so well – not just what she said, but what she could not put into words – that she felt anything was possible.

On the evening after Robbie and Deborah had gone off to see the train they were sitting in the parlour. John had just come in and Martha told him about the masterly telling-off she had given the pair of them.

"Deborah was to blame," she finished. "She knew she was acting in the wrong."

"She's a high-spirited lass," commented John.

"Yes," said Martha, dryly, "too much so at times."

She got up and drew the curtains. The nights were lengthening rapidly and it was almost dark. It was cold too. She shivered, and John, noticing, put a fresh log on the fire and kicked up a blaze. Martha returned to her seat and picked up her sewing. "Deborah wants a father's hand to guide her," she said, sighing slightly. "My sister and her husband died of cholera when she was a babe. It's hard, bringing up a child alone."

John stared into the fire. "Aye. It is," he said. He went on, "You don't get much help from folk round here?"

"Help?" she said scornfully, biting off a thread. "Some are all right but most . . . a narrow-thinking set. Take Amelia Gregory for example."

John looked mystified. "Amelia . . .?"

"An interfering busybody of a woman if ever I knew one," Martha went on crossly. "She's the sort of woman who *has* to poke her nose into other folk's affairs. When I started taking in lodgers she even went and complained to the Squire, Mr Woodward, about me."

"What happened?" asked John.

Martha laughed shortly. "Nothing much. I had to go and see him and he said that navvies were 'a necessary evil'."

John smiled slightly.

"But then he owns shares in the new railway so I didn't expect anything else." She was silent for a moment. "But that doesn't stop Amelia – oh no! She even had the nerve to come round here the other day telling me to have a care to Deborah. I shouldn't allow her – *I* shouldn't if you please – to associate with the likes of . . ." she broke off suddenly and bent her head to her sewing. "No matter," she said uncomfortably, "that woman always upsets me."

". . . with the likes of who, Martha?" said John. "Low-down ruffians like my son?"

"And who gave you leave to use my Christian name, *Mr* Grant?" she replied sharply, drawing herself up straight in her chair.

"Please tell me," said John simply.

Martha put down her sewing. "She saw Deborah and Robbie in the village. They were doing some shopping for me." She looked at him squarely. "That woman is a meddlesome old biddy and I'll thank you to forget I ever mentioned her."

John was watching her with an unfathomable expression on his face. "Why do you take us navvies in?" he asked. "I've worked at building railways nigh on thirteen years and never met anyone like you."

Martha did not speak for a moment, but went on quietly sewing. Then she put her work down and stared into the fire. "My father was a good man," she began quietly. "He brought us up, my sister and I – to believe that we are here to help others. He was so good he'd give away his last farthing to someone in need. And that's just what he did. We didn't know of course when we were little. We just knew that we moved from the nice house with the servants and pretty clothes and toys to a smaller one, and one of the servants left. Then we moved again and more servants left and our clothes weren't so pretty, they were patched and darned, and our toys were old and shabby and we were told to hush when we asked for new ones. So we stopped asking. Then we had no servants and Mother taught us to clean and cook and bake bread and do everything ourselves.

"Finally we moved to this cottage. You should have seen the state it was in when we arrived. There were holes in the ceiling – rotten woodwork – rats. . . ." She paused. The light from the fire cast her profile into sharp relief. John watched her intently.

"Father just didn't notice," she went on. "Mother and I, for my sister was married by then, set to and repaired things as best we could and Father – he would retire to the room he called his 'study' and think and write and then go out and see his friends and give away the remaining money to those in need. He was happy." She sighed, and sat thinking for a moment.

"I remember one day," she said, "it was bitterly cold and we hadn't lit a fire because we'd only the one log left. Mother and I were trying to mend the window. She saw Father turn in to the lane. 'Quick,' she said, 'quick, light the fire. I don't want your father to see us cold. He'd be so upset.' When he came in the one log was burning brightly and the oil lamp glowing. And Mother and I were sitting mending some sheets. He was so pleased – just like a child. He couldn't have borne it if he'd seen us cold – he would have felt such a failure. And all the time a biting wind was blowing from the broken window right down our necks."

She paused for a moment. "He never knew the truth. It killed Mother in the end. The hard work, the cold, the lack of food, the play-acting . . . she was never very strong."

A log fell onto the hearth. Martha got up and replaced it on the fire.

"He doesna' sound like a good man to me," observed John quietly.

"Oh he was," said Martha quickly, "he was. My father was – gentle – and good. Almost unworldly. Mother knew. She understood."

She sat down again and picked up her sewing. "He liked the idea of the railway. He was always fascinated by mechanical things. He wanted to know all about it – how it worked. He went off one day to a locomotive works to see an engine being built. He was only meant to go for the day but he stayed a week and had to borrow the money for his fare home. When he came back he explained it all to me and drew me a picture . . . he used to say that the coming of the railway was the biggest thing that had happened in his lifetime. He thought it would bring a new golden age for rich and poor – cheaper goods, travel . . ." she stopped. "Poor Father. He died before the first piece of earth was dug."

"But why do you . . .?"

"Why do I take in navvies? Well – partly for the money. I wasn't left with much when he died. And you navvies are very well paid – if you don't drink it all away. And then . . . I don't know. Father would have approved and – and I feel sorry for you somehow. . . ."

"You shouldn't," said John shortly. "Most navvies are a bad lot."

"Well – you're away from your home and your kin," she said, "and I get stubborn when everyone is against you and I think . . . 'you can't *all* be bad. . . .'"

She looked up and found John staring at her, his pipe unlit in his hand. She turned pink and stood up quickly, upsetting her work-box. "I must go and see if those children have broken all my china," she said flustered, "I left them washing the dishes." And she hurried out, ignoring the mess on the floor.

John watched her go then looked at the work-box. He got up from his chair, knelt down, and with large, clumsy fingers began laboriously picking up the pins.

9

"I consider it the height of foolishness to be paying the men next week." Mr Fowler's voice carried loudly in the still evening air.

He and Henry Bridgman were wearily riding back after a gruelling day on the railway. Since Mr Fowler's arrival some ten days ago, they had covered many miles both on horseback and by contractor's engine, examining and discussing every detail of the work being done on each section of the line.

To Henry's surprise, Mr Fowler seemed fairly well satisfied with the standard of construction, and said as much, but he was less than satisfied with the progress of the work, and said even more. "You know as well as I," Mr Fowler went on, "that as soon as they get their pay we'll not see them until it's all been drunk and gambled away. And that means yet another delay."

Henry sighed. "There'd be more trouble if we don't pay them," he said wearily. They had already discussed this exhaustively and Henry could see no alternative.

Neither could Mr Fowler, and that made him testy. "I know that – I know that," he replied shortly.

Their voices carried to Tambour Cottage and Robbie looked up from the piece of wood he was whittling in the garden. The two men rode into view. He recognised one of them as the Resident Engineer and the other, older man also seemed vaguely familiar. Mr Fowler glanced at Robbie and recognised him instantly. He stopped.

"You – lad!" he called.

"Me sir?" said Robbie. He got up and limped over to the gate.

"I saw you trying to make the running with that bad foot," said Mr Fowler, "a foolhardy thing to do if ever I saw one."

"Yes, sir," said Robbie.

"But I liked your spirit," went on Mr Fowler, "I like a lad of spirit. How's your foot?"

"Mending, sir."

"Well – keep out of mischief, lad." He turned to go, then looked back. "You read and write?" he asked.

Robbie shook his head. "No, sir."

"Pity," said Mr Fowler. "You learn, and we'll find you a job on the railway when it's open. Eh Mr Bridgman? I'm sure you can arrange something."

He looked at Henry, who nodded, rather bemused at the sudden, unusual behaviour of his employer. "All right lad?" said Mr Fowler. "Learn to read and write."

He turned his horse and both men rode off down the lane, leaving Robbie staring after them. As soon as they were gone, Deborah flew out of the cottage. "Robbie, I heard," she said. "I'll teach you! Then you'll be able to stay with us – I'd like that so much."

Robbie did not speak.

"Aunt's always said you could stay," she went on, "you *will* stay – Robbie?"

He turned away from her with a troubled expression on his face. "I don't know. I can't leave pa," he said, then he opened the gate and limped off down the lane.

He wandered down to the river and sat on the riverbank. It was peaceful down there, peaceful and secluded. He needed to think. Above him towered the great mass of the new rail bridge that was being built across the river, and if he looked up he could see the navvies, like little black ants, swarming all over it. But he did not look up, he looked down into the water and saw fish swimming among the weeds and the clean pebbles of the riverbed.

Deep down inside himself he was scared. Scared of learning to read and write. Scared of a new, altogether different life. He wondered what sort of job he would be offered and whether he would like it or whether he would feel bitter and resentful when he saw the engine drivers roaring past on their marvellous engines.

He tried to think about what it would be like to live in one place all the time, but found it hard to imagine. He wondered what reading and writing were like and if he could ever learn to master them. It had always seemed like some great mystery to look at books with their strange black markings that *meant* something if one only understood. A little knot of excitement stirred at the idea of being able to understand, but he squashed it sternly. "I'd only be duff at it" he said to himself.

He sat picking at the blades of grass as the light was fading. He thought of staying in Arley at Tambour Cottage; of sleeping in the clean white attic room and never going back to the shanty; never sleeping rough, never going on the tramp, begging for food, sleeping in barns, haystacks, ditches. Never being hungry or cold, never having to work until his arms were dropping and his back breaking. He thought of Martha and Deborah. He liked Deborah – most times – and Martha a lot, and if they'd have him stay he could always pay them back when he was working. . . .

Then he thought of his father and there was no decision to make. He could never leave John – he knew that. Even if his father decided to go to India to build railways for the Empire then Robbie would go too. He could not leave him – he was his only relative, the only thing he had in the world; he was . . . the best.

Robbie got up. It was almost dark and he was stiff and cramped. He set off across the fields. He had to find his father, to tell him. . . .

Much later both were sitting in the alehouse, tightly wedged between the packed benches, trying to speak above the noise. His father's reaction wasn't at all what Robbie had expected. "Ye'd be a fool not to take it," said John, angrily banging his fist down on the table, "ye'll no' get a chance like this again – and if Miss Martha's willin' to have you stay. . . ."

"I know that," Robbie said slowly. He stared down at his drink. "I know. And part of me wants to settle . . . an' – an' part of me . . . I don't know. I can't leave you, pa. . . ." It had all seemed so simple down by the river.

John smiled wryly. "Do ye no' trust me on my own?" he asked.

Robbie flushed. "It's not that . . ."

John leaned forward earnestly. "Look Robbie," he said, "ever since your accident I've been thinking. I've done badly by you – very badly."

"Don't say that – you're the best father anyone could have," said Robbie hotly.

John looked down. "That just shows how little you've seen of decent folk," he said. "An' that's ma' own fault. I should never have brought you up to a navvy's life. You've a chance now to get out. Robbie, you've *got* to take it."

The urgency in his voice surprised Robbie. He looked round the smoke-filled room, which was full to overflowing.

Voices were loud and raucous. Next to him a navvy was singing, cheered on by his mates, as he downed mug after mug of ale. In the doorway someone had fallen, and men were cursing and shoving him out of the way as they tried to get in and out of the door. Insensible bodies lay under benches and men danced on the table-tops over them until they, too, fell down dead-drunk. It was dirty, it was sordid . . . it was familiar. Robbie looked back at his father.

"Why haven't *you* got out then?" he demanded. "Why have *you* stuck wi' navvyin' all these years? It's too late, pa – I don't know any other life – I'd be afraid . . .!"

John did not speak for a long while. Then he said quietly: "Look lad – will you give it a try – the readin' and the writin'? Just a try, until the line's done. Then, whatever you decide – I'll no' say a word to make you change your mind. You're your own man now and must do as you think."

Robbie stared down at his glass. He had never felt less like a man and more like a small, frightened boy, but he managed to look at John and grin slightly.

"All right pa – till the line's done," he said, then smiled genuinely, if a bit wryly. "I'll probably be no good at it anyway."

But he was good at it. He was a bright pupil and almost despite himself had very soon mastered the alphabet and could spell out simple words. Deborah threw herself into the task of teaching him with great enthusiasm. She massed together all the books she could find and kept him hard at it for hours at a time. She insisted on him attempting to read everything, even posters and advertisements in shops.

"What does that sign say?" she would ask, pointing to the baker's shop window.

And Robbie would spell out laboriously, "B-U-N-S. Buns?"

They were in the village one day when they saw a poster

being stuck onto a wall. They waited until the man sticking it had gone, then crossed over.

"There's a train," said Robbie, surprised. For at the top of the poster was a small picture of a train.

"Try reading the rest," urged Deborah.

Slowly and with much prompting, Robbie started to read. "Opening of the Se-Sev-Severn V-alley Rail-way. . . ." then he stopped and Deborah continued: "Notice is hereby given that the above Railway will be opened throughout from Shrewsbury to a Junction with the West Midland Railway at Hartlebury, on Saturday the 1st day of February for Passenger and Goods Traffic . . ."

They looked at each other unhappily. "February," said Robbie, "that's not very long."

"No," said Deborah sadly, "it's not," and she shivered suddenly in the cold wind.

They walked home, not speaking.

10

". . . and God shall wipe away all tears from their eyes; and there shall be no more – death, n-neither sorrow, nor c-crying, neither shall there be any more pain: for – for the former – things are passed away." Robbie looked up triumphantly from the Bible lying open in front of him. "How was that?" he said.

"Very good, Robbie," replied Deborah who was sitting beside him following every word. "Wasn't it Aunt?"

Martha did not reply. She had seen John come quietly to the doorway and stand still while Robbie was reading. She had seen the intense look of pride on his face as he had watched his son and then she had seen him suddenly turn and hurry away and she was wondering just why he had gone.

"Read some more," urged Deborah, and Robbie obediently bent his head once more to the Bible.

Deborah was working Robbie as hard as she could in the hope that the more he learnt in the short time left, the more difficult it would be for him to return to being a navvy.

Robbie was progressing well both in reading and writing.

He was progressing well in other ways, since his foot had improved tremendously. So much so that one cold, frosty afternoon he proudly emerged from the doctor's house in the village aided only by a stick.

Martha and Deborah met him outside the doctor's. "Where's your crutch Robbie?" demanded Deborah.

"Broken up – used for firewood – given to someone else . . . I don't know!" Robbie replied happily.

"That's a very fine stick," said Martha, "mind you take care of it."

"It's one of the Doctor's own," said Robbie, walking carefully on the slippery road.

"It makes you look quite the gentleman," said Deborah, looking at him critically. That made Robbie and Martha laugh and they were laughing as they turned the corner into the main street.

At the far end of the street, slowly walking towards them were three navvies. They were walking as though they were very weary, and all three were caked with mud from top to toe.

"Pa!" called Robbie, recognising John, and he hurried to meet him.

John's face lit up with pleasure, but when he saw Martha and Deborah following Robbie, he looked down at his filthy clothes and felt acutely uncomfortable. "I'll see you at home Robbie lad," he mumbled, "I can't walk wi' you like this. . . ."

His two companions exchanged glances and Baldy grinned. "Come for a jar instead," urged Spider, "we're not proud." Baldy laughed.

Martha and Deborah reached the group. "Good afternoon Mr Grant," said Martha composedly. She looked at the men and quickly summed up the situation. "If you're on your way home for tea Mr Grant, I'm afraid it'll be late. It was

Robbie's fault. He couldn't be dragged away from the doctor's."

"I'm doin' without the crutch now pa," chimed in Robbie eagerly, "and the Doctor lent me this stick."

There was a moment's awkward silence. Spider and Baldy exchanged further glances. "Be seein' you Giant," Spider said finally and he and Baldy went off in the direction of the alehouse.

Martha smiled at John. "We'd be grateful for a hand with these baskets, wouldn't we Deborah?" she said.

"Aye. Oh aye, of course," said John, watching the two navvies disappear round the corner. He hastily took the proffered baskets and the four of them walked up the street to the church, Robbie and Deborah chattering in front, John and Martha silent behind.

They passed two ladies and Martha nodded graciously at them. "Good afternoon Miss Gregory, Miss James," she said. The ladies stared at John and did not reply.

"That'll give them something to talk about, silly old tabbies," muttered Martha savagely.

John stopped. "It's no' right I should be walkin' with you – it's only causing trouble. . . ."

"Stuff and nonsense," replied Martha with a martial gleam in her eye.

John looked at her, then suddenly smiled. "I wouldna' like to get on the wrong side of you Martha," he said, "you scare me half to death."

Martha looked at him quickly. There he was, walking beside her, completely dwarfing her, the big, bearded giant of a man, absurdly carrying two tiny wickerwork baskets in his great dirty calloused hands as if they had been precious porcelain.

She wanted to laugh, then, as suddenly, she wanted to cry. She said abruptly: "And who gave you leave to use my Christian name, *Mr* Grant?" and they smiled at each other as if sharing some private joke before looking quickly away and hurrying to catch up with Robbie and Deborah.

That evening Martha found it difficult to sit in the parlour composedly sewing with John sitting opposite, his eyes fixed intently on her. She found to her disgust that her hands were trembling as she tried to thread a needle. "Drat!" she exclaimed at the fourth attempt.

"Martha . . ." said John suddenly.

"I've always said that when I can't thread my own needles I must be getting old," she said hurriedly.

"Martha . . ." said John again.

She could not look at him. She was too flustered. "You fool," she thought to herself, "you fool, you're behaving like some green girl of sixteen." She folded up her sewing and sat quietly.

"Yes?" she said.

John did not speak for a moment and Martha waited, outwardly calm.

"Ye're not old," John finally blurted out.

Martha managed a smile, then threaded her needle and picked up her sewing. John continued to stare at her.

"It's payday tomorrow," he said abruptly. 'I'll settle up with you then."

Martha froze. "You're thinking of leaving?" she said in a tight voice that she would not keep from trembling.

"No," said John earnestly, "oh no." He got up and went over to the window. "There's something I've been meaning to say – to ask. . . ." he said to the curtains.

"Yes?"

"But I'll settle my debts wi' you first," he went on firmly, turning to her as he spoke. "Ye'll be here – in the evening?"

"When am I not?" she said, trying to speak lightly.

"Aye. Well." He went to the door. "Tomorrow evening then."

"I'll have something special for tea," she said.

"Aye – do that – something special," he replied and walked out of the door.

Martha took a deep breath and went back to her sewing.

The next day was crisp and bright. At noon a horn sounded, echoing from end to end along the railway. There was an instant response. Tools were dropped, work halted and waggons left as the men began to race away from the line. John's voice checked them momentarily. "Back on Thursday lads – and sober!"

Ironic jeers greeted this, and in a very short time the cutting was deserted. John looked round at the pick-axes, the shovels, the rocks, the heaps of ballast, the stack of sleepers and the neat piles of shining new rails ready to be laid and he picked up his jacket and followed the men off the site.

He went into the shanty town and made his way to a large barrel used to collect rainwater. The shanty was deserted. John put down his jacket, took off his shirt and immersed his head and shoulders in the water. Then he dried himself roughly on his shirt before putting it on. He picked up his jacket and rifled through the pockets. From one he took out a fresh handkerchief which he tied round his neck and from the other emerged a brand new plush waistcoat, purple with silver buttons. He looked at it critically then put it on. He spent some time combing his hair with a comb that had lost most of its teeth and finally he took his white felt hat and damped, brushed and pummelled it into some sort of shape before sticking it firmly on his head. He was humming to himself as he walked out of the shanty in the direction of the Tommy Shop.

A table had been placed in front of the shop and behind it sat Mr Peters, the timekeeper, and two men. There were piles of coins and several long lists on the table and a vast number of navvies milling round in front, forming a loose sort of queue that stretched down almost as far as the river.

There was a general holiday atmosphere as the men waited to be paid, with much joking, chatting and drinking. Shorty stood in the doorway to his shop, grinning vacuously at everything and everyone. On these occasions he commandeered the services of several small boys as helpers while he played the genial host, talking and laughing with the men as they went straight from the table, pockets jingling with money, to his shop, to emerge some time later with empty pockets but staggering under the weight of the food and drink they carried.

John joined the end of the queue.

"Ye're lookin' smart Giant," Spider commented. "What's the occasion?"

"Why man, it's payday i'n't it?" John replied. "That's occasion enough."

"Not if you're like me," Spider said gloomily. "I've drunk most of this month's pay already. I owe all of it to that one-armed rogue over there to pay for last month's drink." He shook his fist in mock anger at Shorty who responded by grinning widely and shrugging his shoulders.

"Ye'll still have enough to go on the randy tonight if I know aught of you Spider," said John laughing, and the queue slowly moved forwards. He saw Robbie in the distance looking round. "Robbie! Over here lad!" he called.

"Hello Pa. My, you're spruced up."

"Just what I told him," said Spider. "Looks like he's dressed up for a weddin' or somethin'."

John ignored this. "Mind here awhile and we'll go to the alehouse," he said. "I've something I want to talk about."

"I doubt there's much room in the alehouse pa," said Robbie.

Robbie was right. The alehouse was packed tight with navvies and more and more were pouring in through the doors. John and Robbie pushed their way through the crowds. "It's goin' to be some randy tonight lad," shouted John above the noise.

"Aye," Robbie called back. "When I came through the village there was folks putting up shutters early."

John concentrated on getting drinks and then they elbowed their way into a corner. Thankfully they sat down and sipped their drinks in silence. Both were preoccupied with their own thoughts.

"Pa," said Robbie suddenly.

"Aye?"

"You shouldn't have paid for the doctor for me. I'll – I'll pay you back when I'm working."

"There's no need," John replied absently.

"Doctor said I'd be fit in a week or two," said Robbie.

"I'm glad."

"Will you take me on then?"

"No, Robbie." John was positive.

"Why?" asked Robbie, his hands tightly grasped round his mug.

John looked at him. "Ye'd no' stand the pace, that's why. Not the way it is now. Could you lift over twenty tons o' muck a day – at least? Are ye fit for that?"

"I'd soon pick up."

"Oh, I know you're a keen worker. But ye're out of trim – you must know that." John stopped for a moment. "And what about the learning?"

"What about it?"

"I heard you was getting on fine with the reading and writing."

"So?"

"There's a future in that. There's no' much of a future in navvyin'." John paused. "Won't you consider that job Mr Fowler offered . . .?" he said tentatively. Robbie looked down and did not speak. John watched him for a moment, then took a deep breath.

"Robbie – that brings me – to what I was wantin' to say," he broke off and cleared his throat. "Robbie – lad – would it make a difference – if I was to tell you I was thinkin' of settlin' down myself? If I was to tell you that I'm goin' from here to ask Miss Martha if she and I could be wed? How would you feel then?"

Robbie slowly raised his head and looked at John with astonishment.

"You mustn't . . . you're doin' it for me . . ."

John suddenly laughed. "You're far an' away out laddie – I'm doin' it for myself. He looked at Robbie. "Robbie – are you *sure* you don't mind . . .?"

Robbie smiled. A slow smile to start with, getting broader and broader until his whole face was alight. He felt light-headed. He felt he wanted to get up on the table, lame as he was, and dance and sing. . . . He felt. . . .

"Mind?" he said. "Oh pa . . .!"

II

Down in the village there was singing and dancing. There was also fighting, swearing and drinking. Gangs of navvies roamed the streets, picking quarrels with one another or with any stray villager they happened to meet. The villagers scurried into their houses, securely bolted the doors behind them and worried about what the night would bring, and the navvies, thwarted, banged on the doors and shouted curses up at the windows.

A group of them called out to Deborah as she ran from the garden to the shelter of the cottage. Once inside, she met Martha coming down the stairs. "Mind you secure all the downstairs windows now, Deborah!" said Martha.

Deborah stopped still in amazement. Aunt was wearing her best dress, her very best dress, the one she wore only on Christmas Day and other special occasions.

"Do you heed me Deborah!" asked Martha sharply.

"Yes aunt," said Deborah and went off in the direction of the kitchen, still wondering.

"Though why folks have to spend all their pay on drink as soon as they get it, I'll never know," said Martha, half to herself as she opened the door to the parlour. She walked to the table and stood looking down at it with satisfaction. She really had made a very nice tea she thought, a special tea. She threw another log on the fire. Never mind the expense, she thought recklessly, this is an occasion.

It was fast getting dark but in the shanty town the great roaring fires that had been lit served as well as the daylight. The place was teeming with life. Every hut, every shack seemed to be bursting with people intent on enjoying payday to the hilt. Parties were taking place at every corner, huge affairs with singing, dancing and music (provided by accordians, violins and even penny whistles) to go with the abundance of food and drink. Everyone was smiling, everyone was laughing, everyone was happy, and if the firelight showed up some premature wrinkles or ragged clothes it did not matter. Not on payday. Groups of men, arms flung round each other, swayed along the paths, calling out to their friends; children laughed and chased each other round the fires, stealing the best bits of roasting beef and fighting over the empty bottles before drinking the dregs; women emerged from the huts, gay scarves round their hair, red-faced, carrying steaming cauldrons of stew.

The shanty was warm and friendly and no one there was immune from feeling part of one giant family caught up in some massive celebration. Robbie felt it as he and John picked their way through the twisting lanes, avoiding getting caught up in great happy parties. He looked round and a rush of homesickness for the shanty came over him, and he knew when he looked at his father that John felt the same. They walked on and did not speak.

Suddenly their way was barred. Navvies from John's butty were standing, supporting each other, grinning foolishly at them. They closed in and Spider caught hold of John's jacket. "I've spent it Giant. This month's . . . and next month's. . . ." He staggered, and John held him up.

"Are ye comin' to have a jar with us Giant?" wheezed Carrot-Top, while Fat-Gut banged him on the shoulder and Topper solemnly shook his hand.

"I've more important things to do," said John.

Spider started to sob. "More important than drinkin' with your butty?" he cried. "Your very own mates . . ."

John gently pushed him off. "Aye Spider," he said, "another time."

"But we'd not take it kindly if you don't have a jar with us." Green-Eye stood in his path. It was quite dark and neither Robbie nor John could see him clearly. "Now would we lads?" he went on, and held out a full bottle to John.

John looked round the waiting butty slowly, an inscrutable expression on his face, then he turned to Robbie. "You get home an' tell Martha I'll no' be long. I must have one jar wi' the lads." A cheer went up from the navvies. Robbie hesitated. "Go on," said John, giving him a push. 'I'll no' be long, I promise."

The butty, John in their midst, turned down a lane and were soon lost to view. Robbie stared after them, then slowly started off in the direction of the cottage. He felt somehow uncomfortable at returning without his father. He shrugged his shoulders. Pa'll be along straight away, he thought, but his feet dragged, and a slight sense of unease lessened the warm happy feeling he had had since hearing John's news.

He half-expected his father to catch him up along the way but he reached the cottage alone and stepped into the parlour. The first thing he saw was Martha half-starting out of her chair, a shy smile of pleasure on her face, changing instantly to one of disappointment which she immediately concealed under her usual calm.

"Oh. Robbie," she said.

"Where's Mr Grant?" Deborah asked and he noticed that the table was loaded down with the fine tea. He blinked at the size and magnificence of the spread, and Deborah asked him again, more insistently: "Where's Mr Grant, Robbie?"

"He'll no' be long. He had to stay a wee while." Robbie felt a strong urge to justify John. "He said to tell you he had to have a drink with the lads. Just one, quick, drink. It was expected of him. He said he'll no' be long. . . ." He trailed off into silence.

"Well," said Martha in much her usual way. "We'll sit and wait for him. Come and warm yourself by the fire Robbie, and perhaps you'd care to read to us?"

The reading was not a success. He stumbled and stuttered and Deborah seemed too listless to correct him. Martha was clearly not listening at all and Robbie eventually lapsed into silence. He looked at Martha and was struck by how pretty she looked.

"That's – that's a nice dress Miss Martha," he said shyly.

Martha looked at him, a bit sadly. "Thank you Robbie," she said. "It's – only an old thing." She got up hurriedly and went out of the room. When she returned she had changed into her everyday dress and her manner, too, was changed. "You must be starving," she said briskly. "We won't wait tea any longer."

They ate what they could of the special tea then sat for a long time while the food congealed and the tea went cold. The long evening dragged on.

The plates banged together as Martha jumped up and started to clear away the remains of the tea. Deborah was drawing patterns in the sugar bowl and Robbie was staring out of the window. It was very late. Apart from the occasional band of drunken men passing down the lane, everywhere was quiet and still. The clock struck twelve.

"Deborah – time you were in bed. You too Robbie."

Martha spoke sharply and smacked Deborah's hand away from the sugar.

"But Mr Grant isn't back," said Deborah, transferring her attentions to the crumbs of bread on the table.

"Well, that's nothing to do with you child – and will you stop playing with the food!" Martha said exasperated.

"But he said he'd not be long – didn't he Robbie?"

Robbie did not reply. Martha glanced at him then swept the cloth from the table. "Bed," she said.

After they had gone Martha sat for hours over the dying fire, hoping every minute to see John standing in the doorway, penitent, with some good reason for being late. As the night wore on she began to worry. Distant sounds of rioting men could sometimes be heard and Martha imagined John lying in a ditch after being attacked by drunken navvies. She imagined him cut, bleeding, helpless in that dreadful shanty town. I must find him, she thought and she took down her cloak and was half-way down the garden path before she realised what she was doing.

She stopped still. The noise was louder here and on the horizon, in the direction of the shanty, the sky glowed red. Abruptly she turned and went back inside, bolting and barring the front door behind her.

Let him stay out all night if he dares to come home, she thought angrily as she went upstairs. She laughed bitterly at her own stupidity. To think of him being attacked by drunken navvies indeed – why should he, when he was one himself? She reached her room and started to undress. Her best dress hung in front of the wardrobe.

What a fool – what a stupid fool, she thought to herself. "You ought to be ashamed of yourself, Martha Puddyfoot," she said as she thrust her best dress viciously away. Well, I've learned my lesson, she thought. I'll never allow myself to behave like that again.

She got into bed and blew out the candle. I'll carry on with the lodgers because of the money, but as for invitations to share my private parlour in the evening never again, she thought. And as for Mr Grant. . . . She turned over and found, to her disgust, that her pillow was wet.

Upstairs in his attic room Robbie was not sleeping. He lay in bed, hour after hour, eyes open, ears straining for the least sound. There was nothing. He stared at the row of disapproving dolls. Why? he thought, *Why?* But the dolls only stared back at him, unblinking. He got up and turned their faces to the wall, then went back to bed and dozed fitfully.

Towards dawn he could stay in bed no longer. He went over to the window, pulled back the curtains and looked out. It was just beginning to get light and a fine rain was falling. Robbie dressed quickly and quietly let himself out of the house.

The aftermath of the randy was apparent even in the village, where broken bottles were strewn across the street and a couple of navvies were lying in the gutter, bottles clasped in their hands, snoring loudly. The ferryman was nowhere to be seen, but there was a small boat drawn up to the jetty. Quickly Robbie untied it, got in, and cast off from the bank.

Across the river it was worse. Robbie walked over the fields, passing inert bodies lying where they had fallen. The shanty town was grey in the early light and a few spirals of grey smoke drifted up from the remains of the bonfires. People lay everywhere, dead drunk and asleep and Robbie picked his way slowly, going from group to group, examining each person before moving on. The rain put out the last of the fires and dripped off the roofs of the huts on to the men lying in the mud. Scavenging dogs and cats were feasting on the remains of the food and a rat ran over a man huddled in a corner. Robbie shuddered and walked on, through every lane, into every hut.

He searched all over the shanty town, but his father was not there. He had found men from John's butty, sprawled over, under and round a table, but they were so drunk that they had not stirred even when he had called and shaken them.

Robbie left the shanty and went down to the line. The rain was falling steadily now and it was just light enough to see the deserted waggons, the outlines of the tools abandoned the previous day, and the massive earth works. He started at one end of the vast cutting and carefully limped along its length. There was no one there. It was utterly silent, utterly deserted.

Then he stopped abruptly and listened. Heavy, irregular breathing was coming from over to the left. Robbie moved swiftly to a waggon and walked round. There was his father, lying in a hollow, half-propped against the side of the waggon, eyes closed. He was wet through and coated with mud. His handkerchief was untied, his new waistcoat torn and his hat gone. Robbie stood still and watched him.

John half-opened his eyes and groaned. "Bad ale . . . I mighta' known . . ." He winced at the early morning light and closed his eyes. Robbie made no sound but suddenly John looked up and stared straight at him. "Robbie? What are you doin' here?"

There was a long silence. Robbie said curtly, "Lookin' for you."

John blinked. "I'm sorry. . . ."

"You said you'd come soon. You said you were going to ask Miss Martha to wed . . . why . . .?"

John held his hands to his head. "My head. . . ." He paused for a moment and looked at Robbie. "I *had* to go for one jar . . . only one . . . I didna' mean to stay . . . it was bad ale. . . ."

Robbie turned abruptly. John caught his arm. "Robbie – I'm no' the big hero you make out. I never was . . . I tried to tell you. . . ." Robbie shook himself free and limped off without a word. "It'll be all right Robbie!" John called after him. 'I'll explain to Martha. . . ." but Robbie had gone.

Some hours later the explanations were not coming so easily. John was standing uneasily in the parlour confronted by a total stranger – a small, icily cold and unbearably polite Martha. His excuses were brushed aside. "It is of no consequence to me how you spend your pay Mr Grant. I don't want to hear any more."

"But Martha. . . ."

"I have *not* given you leave to use my Christian name, Mr Grant!"

This was no private joke to be shared. Martha was absolutely serious, desperately unhappy and furiously angry. She had difficulty keeping her emotions under control.

"Och, I'm doin' this all wrong," said John, holding his throbbing head in his hands. "My head's spinning so."

"You must think me foolish," said Martha quietly and coldly. "We've had navvies in this village for nigh on three years and it's always the same." Her voice rose. "Come payday and it's off on a randy, and drink and riot until it's all spent. I did think you different, but you're not. . . ." She stopped, fighting down the anger and bitterness she was feeling.

John took a step towards her. "Martha. . . ."

"*Don't call me that!*" she screamed, suddenly unable to contain herself. "You're just – just a lawless, Godforsaken bunch living on the outside of decent Christian communities."

"That's no' true . . ." John retorted, stung.

"It *is* the truth, so help me," she replied passionately. "You've no settled life – you tramp from job to job . . . you're known by outlandish names – I'll warrant no vicar ever christened you Giant – no, and from all I've heard you don't even wed in the sight of God, but only in the sight of a drunken mob by jumping over a broomstick. You're . . . you're nothing but savages and I want no more to do with you!" She stopped, horrified at herself. She was shaking uncontrollably and gripped the edge of the table for support.

John was quite white and his eyes were glazed. He was looking straight at Martha, almost through her, to something that was not in the room. When he spoke, it was with a great effort, as if every word was wrenched out of him, and his voice was harsh.

"Jeannie MacDonald and I were wed in the sight of God at the Kirk at Shieldaig. Jeannie died giving birth to Robbie's sister when he was two years old. The bairn died ten days after." He stopped and there was a moment's silence. "Jeannie and I grew up together. She died in my arms. After she died I couldna' stay in the Highlands. I couldna' stay any place long. I took up wi' navvyin' so I could keep movin'." He stopped again and swallowed hard. "I've never spoken of Jeannie until now. I've never even told Robbie. It – hurt – too much. Even now. After all these years. . . ." He stopped again.

"Mr Grant. . . ." Martha spoke almost in a whisper.

John focused on her and the glazed look went from his eyes, but his face was deeply lined and he looked old – old and tired. "No," he said, "hear me out." He paused for a moment. "There's been no woman for me since Jeannie died. Until you. I was coming to ask you to marry me but I was pressed to stop for a drink – only one. . . ." He stopped again. "You're a fine woman, Martha . . . an' I'm no' good enough for you. I can see that now." He sighed wearily. "I'll pack my things an' no' trouble you further."

He turned away and walked out of the room. Martha stood clutching onto the table, and watched him go.

12

After leaving John lying in the cutting Robbie went straight down to the river and sat on the edge of the bank in his favourite secluded spot near the bridge. He stared down at the water and tried to think, but nothing made sense any more. He just felt cold, sick and unreal.

He caught a glimpse of Deborah in the distance, running up the path, obviously searching for him, and he looked round for some means of escape but there wasn't any and by this time she had seen him. She came nearer, and he saw that her face was blotched and red from crying and her hair in a tangled mess.

"Robbie," she called out as she ran up, "oh Robbie it's awful – *do* something!"

Robbie turned his back on her. "It's nothin' to do with me," he said coldly.

Deborah caught her breath on a sob. "But he's your father!"

"He's no' the father I thought I had," Robbie said bitterly.

Deborah knelt beside him. "Because he got drunk you mean?" she asked.

"Lord no," he said scornfully. "I must have seen him drunk a thousand times, an' in a worse state after."

"Well, what?" Deborah said, mystified.

Robbie did not speak for a moment. He bent his head. "I'm ashamed of him," he said quietly.

"But he's packing," said Deborah urgently. "He's going – you *can't* let him go! And Aunt's crying – she's in the kitchen crying and she *never* cries!"

"I'm sorry," Robbie said indifferently.

Deborah stood up. "Aren't you going to do *anything*?" she demanded.

Robbie shrugged his shoulders.

"You stupid thing," she said vehemently, "you stupid, selfish thing!"

Robbie looked up, more surprised than angry.

"I hate you," Deborah went on fiercely, "everybody does things for you and you don't do anything for anyone. Mr Grant looked after you when you were ill and paid the doctor . . ."

"I'll pay him back," Robbie broke in, stung and getting angry in turn.

". . . and all you do is – is wander round feeling sorry for yourself and let everyone run after you. . . ."

"That's not true!" Robbie flung back at her. "I'm going back to work as soon as I can!"

Deborah paid no attention. "And Aunt takes care of you and – and I've been teaching you to read and write because I liked you and hoped you'd stay – but I don't now. I hope you go. I don't ever want to see you again!"

"And I don't want to see you either!" Robbie shouted back. "You're just a silly little girl and you don't understand anything!"

"I understand this," she said furiously. "Your father's a

good man and Aunt loves him and – and – if you won't do anything I'll – I'll never speak to you again! Ever!"

With that she burst into fresh tears and ran off. Robbie stared after her, seething. His first impulse was to run and catch her up and shout back at her. How dare she, silly little girl that she was, years younger than him, speak to him like that? How dare she! Silly little thing, so frightened the first time she saw a train that she dived head-first into the bushes! He began to feel better. He wasn't selfish – it wasn't true – she just didn't understand anything. He didn't expect people to do things for him . . . it wasn't *his* fault he'd hurt his foot. . . .

As he sat, his anger slowly subsided and doubts began to creep in. Suddenly he got up and limped off. He went as fast as he could back to Tambour Cottage and reached the garden gate just as his father was coming down the path. John was carrying a bundle, an old blanket he always used on the tramp with his possessions tied up inside, and a stout stick.

"Pa! Pa – where are you going?" Robbie called, running to him.

John opened the gate. "Back where I belong," he said shortly.

Robbie clutched his arm. "Don't go . . . please. . . ."

"There's nothin' for me here," John said with finality. He came through the gate and started walking off down the road. Robbie ran alongside, and John glanced sideways at him. "You can come along or stay as you please – it doesna' make much difference either way."

Robbie kept hold of his arm. "Please don't go," he pleaded, "please – she loves you – Deborah said she's in there cryin' and she never cries. . . . please. . . ."

John stopped and stood irresolutely in the middle of the road. He stared at Robbie then turned and looked at the cottage. Abruptly he thrust his bundle at Robbie and strode back in through the garden gate. Robbie sighed with relief and slowly began to follow.

John went into the house. The kitchen door was open and the smell of fresh baked bread filled the house. He could see Martha at the oven, carefully lifting out the loaves one by one. She turned to the table, saw John and dropped the bread on the floor. Her face was red and flushed and tears were rolling unheeded down her cheeks. "Martha . . .?" John said uncertainly, stopping in the doorway.

Martha lifted her hand to wipe away the tears. "I'm sorry," she whispered, "I'm so sorry. . . ."

John walked into the kitchen and took her in his arms. He held her tightly and stroked her hair and Martha closed her eyes and felt at peace.

They decided on a quiet wedding to be held straight after the opening of the railway. It could not be sooner as Martha had to make her wedding dress, and John felt obliged to see the work on the line through to the end.

They went to church to see the Vicar and there was quite a stir in the small village community when it became known that Martha Puddyfoot was going to wed one of the railway navvies.

"I never expected any different after she started taking them navvies in as her lodgers," sniffed Amelia Gregory, and her friend, Miss James, agreed. Martha was fairly generally criticised for her intended action and ladies of the village who made such things their business wore a path to her door in an attempt to show her the error of her ways and persuade her not to go ahead with what could only be a disastrous marriage.

The first Sunday the banns were read the church was more than usually crowded with people straining – politely – to catch a glimpse of the large bearded man sitting quietly beside Martha, but to their disappointment he behaved quite normally and did not do anything outrageous. Robbie squirmed under the stares and Deborah giggled, but

John and Martha were only amused and unconcerned.

As they went out after the service the Vicar shook John warmly by the hand. "It would be very good to see some of your fellow workmen here on Sundays, Mr Grant," he said.

John smiled. "That's no' very likely Vicar," he replied. "Most of them work Sundays. Indeed I'm workin' myself later today."

A small crowd had gathered round them. "I'm sorry to hear it," said the Vicar, "perhaps you can persuade them otherwise."

"What's that you're sorry to hear Vicar?" said a portly gentleman, inclined to be deaf. "Capital sermon by the way."

The Vicar inclined his head at the compliment. "Thank you Mr Greavey. Mr Grant here was saying that the railway navigators have to work on Sundays, which of course accounts for their absence from church."

Amelia Gregory, hovering on the edge of the group, snorted, "You wouldn't get those heathen to step foot inside a church, work or no! But Martha knows my feelings on *that* matter."

"Yes, indeed Amelia," Martha replied sweetly, "You spoke *very* plainly to me the other day."

"Ladies, ladies," interposed the Vicar mildly. "Miss Amelia, we must not judge too harshly. What about our friend Mr Grant here? The railway workers are the Lord's creatures, doing His work."

As the four walked off through the churchyard Deborah asked suddenly, "Why do navvies have to work on the Lord's day?"

Robbie shrugged his shoulders. "They don't always. It depends on the company who owns the railway and the contractor who's undertaken to build it. But if there's a deadline for the opening it just means working all hours."

"But that's a sin, surely?" Deborah asked.

Robbie smiled slightly. "God's wonderful railways must be built," he said mockingly, "and the pay's good."

The deadline for the opening of the Severn Valley railway meant that for the next two weeks they saw little of John at Tambour Cottage. The pressure was on, and John and the rest of the navvies were working round the clock in the rush to get the line finished.

"Come on you rogues, put your backs into it!" John called to his butty.

"It's a killin' pace you've set already Giant," grumbled Spider.

"It's no' the work'll kill you Spider, it's the drink," John replied, to the laughter of the other navvies. He went on in a louder voice. "You muckshifters had better get this finished faster than you can think. Ye're keeping me from my wedding!"

A cheer went up at that and the work progressed. The last of the massive earth works were finished and the trackbed levelled. A layer of ballast was laid to a depth of about twelve inches to allow for drainage and provide suppleness to the completed railroad. The ballast consisted of rough stones and chippings with a layer of coarse gravel on top, and was taken from local quarries. Then the wooden sleepers were placed horizontally and bedded down with more ballast and finally the shining new rails of the permanent way were laid vertically and firmly spiked down through the sleepers and into the ballast with iron spikes.

Gangs of workmen were employed on all the other parts of the railway: stations were built; platforms constructed; station buildings with their waiting rooms, ticket offices, booking offices, lamp rooms, sheds, sidings, houses to accommodate the stationmaster and his family – the whole forty-four miles of the new railway hummed with activity.

The number of accidents increased. John Crosby, known as Shropshire John because he came from Bridgnorth, was one of a group working all night to build new sidings at Buildwas Station when he was run over by an engine and killed. Curly Twist had both arms broken when a boulder fell on him, Hawkeye Jones lost a foot under a length of rail and an engine ran off the line at Stourport causing damage to the track but injuring no one.

More and more locomotives were to be seen, testing the new track and running supplies here and there as needed. The contractor's engine ran constantly with either Mr Bridgman or his colleagues on the footplate, and Mr Fowler spent more and more time at the line, tirelessly examining, inspecting and checking every mile of track.

Henry Bridgman had not seen his bed for some nights and was haggard and worn. As he and Mr Fowler were bumped and jolted along the very last stretch of the temporary way before it was finally lifted, he thankfully reflected that he would never again have to ride on such a nerve-shattering road. The rails laid at the start of any new railway works were terrifying to travel on, and he had had to develop a strong stomach for the steep climbs and descents and hair-raising bends and turns along the rough road.

They lurched round a corner at high speed and Henry watched in dismay as Mr Fowler, who had borrowed Henry's thick winter coat, inadvertently dropped it off the footplate. It had been given him by his wife on his last birthday and Henry swallowed hard as he saw it being torn to shreds under the wheels.

The problems mounted. The brand-new locomotives, ordered months before, were nowhere near ready, and the Oldbury Carriage Building Company who were building some of the new coaches were having problems with obtaining supplies of wood. It was becoming impossible to enter Henry's office for the mountain of paperwork inside and for days at a stretch he did not have time to set foot there.

In the towns and villages along the route excitement

mounted. A meeting was held by the principal inhabitants of Bridgnorth to discuss the manner in which the opening of the railway was to be celebrated. The Mayor proposed a public dinner and a ball to mark the event and this was agreed. It was also agreed to hand out free coal to the needy of the town and hold a great open-air feast for them.

Not to be outdone, the inhabitants of Bewdley held a meeting too and also decided on a dinner and a ball. The meeting at the Town Hall was crowded with local tradesmen and other worthies of the town and great support for the new railway was shown.

As Mr Nicholls, one of the main speakers, put it: "I am quite satisfied that the opening of the Severn Valley line will be beneficial to the trade of Bewdley and will be the promise of better days to come in the future for this town. We will then be like other towns – we'll be able to go ahead like other places and not continue to be looked upon and spoken of as 'little' Bewdley." There was a roar of agreement and Mr Nicholls expanded. "I can tell some of the big places that 'little' Bewdley is a better place in many respects. We can afford to buy some of them and give them away afterwards!" The roars and cheers increased and another open-air feast for the poor was agreed on.

Arley was working itself up into a fever pitch of excitement, especially when Squire Woodward declared a holiday for the workers on his estate the day the railway opened, with a free meal of bread, roast pig and ale.

Victoria Bridge, declared an "engineering wonder" by a local paper, attracted a steady stream of reporters, engineers and other interested people who turned up in the village in order to see this "extraordinary piece of iron work" – as another newspaper put it. As the bridge was barely half a mile from Arley the village grew quite proud of their "wonder" and villagers could be seen strolling out in the evening to marvel at it.

The inhabitants of Tambour Cottage were also busy. Robbie had accompanied Martha and Deborah to Kidderminster to choose and purchase material for her wedding dress and Deborah's bridesmaid's dress. The parlour became full of cut-out pieces of fine material with pins sticking out to prick the unwary.

They saw very little of John. He came and went at odd times, snatching an hour or two's sleep as he could, together with a slice of pie or a piece of tart. His face was grey and lined with exhaustion, and when he looked at the patterns for the dresses and fingered the soft material he said all the right things but his mind was not really on weddings. "I'll need a week's sleep first Martha, love," he said, "otherwise I'll disgrace you by snoring at the altar."

Martha was worried, as far as she could be worried when she was so happy. "It's not right to work men that hard," she said, but Robbie understood. Work was always hard towards the end of a job, especially as there were fewer and fewer men around.

For the navvies had begun to drift away – in ones, in twos, in groups – so quietly that the villagers hardly noticed how the shanty was shrinking daily and the alehouses no longer monopolised by hard-drinking navvies. Robbie understood, for he and John had rarely stayed to the very end of a job. Lured by the whiff of something new with good pay, he and John would have been off on the tramp long ago. Well, that was all over, and Robbie had other things on his mind. The next day was to be an important one in his life.

13

The next day found Robbie standing in a long line of well-scrubbed, neatly pressed, shining young men. Like the others he was dressed in his best suit and trying not to let his nervousness show too much. They were standing in a corridor, a formidable corridor with plush carpet on the floor and heavy pictures of grim-faced men on the walls. The line ended in front of a closed door. Every now and then it would open and a grim-faced man would beckon the next in the queue forward into the room beyond. The door would shut behind them and Robbie wondered where they went to as they never came out the same way.

Martha had lent Robbie her pony and trap but he had had to get up at five in order to make the journey to Worcester to the Railway Company's headquarters in good time. John had been working all night and Robbie had not seen him that morning but Martha had insisted on getting up to make him a hearty breakfast before he left.

The journey in the cold morning light had awakened

many memories, for it was the same road he was now jogging down in such well-fed, warm comfort that he had limped along in pain and discomfort all those months ago. Now he could even do without his stick, although the doctor said he would always have a slight limp. How kind he had been, he thought, how kind everyone had been. If only he could get a job with the new railway he could in some way repay all of them.

The queue moved forwards and Robbie found himself next in line, staring at the closed door. It opened and the grim man stuck his head out and beckoned him. Robbie straightened his jacket, felt for the letters in his pocket then walked in. The door closed behind.

Inside, the room was even more opulent than the corridor. The coat of arms of the Company was on one wall with a large, highly-polished desk beneath it. Behind the desk sat two men. They nodded curtly as Robbie nervously handed over his letters. Silence fell as the older man quickly read them and passed them to the other man. Robbie twisted his hat in his hands. Mr Hartwell, the older man, leant back in his chair and scrutinised Robbie in silence. "How old are you?" he said eventually.

"F-fifteen, sir," Robbie stuttered.

"And what sort of employment would you like with the Company?"

"I don't know sir," Robbie said, "anything." He paused. "I'm a bit lame though. . . ."

Mr Hartwell picked up one of the letters. "So I see from this letter from Doctor Williams," he said. He picked up the other letter and studied both of them. "Mmm. And Mr Bridgman has passed on a recommendation from Mr Fowler. . . ." He looked over the letters at Robbie: "You do have some influential friends, my lad."

Robbie's heart sank, but then he realised that Mr Hartwell was smiling. Well, not exactly smiling, but there was a smile in his voice and Robbie was suddenly not too frightened any more.

"Well then, let me see . . ." Mr Hartwell doodled on a clean pad of paper . . . "health good, other than your leg?"

"Oh yes, sir," said Robbie.

Mr Hartwell turned to the man beside him. "Anything suitable Jones?" he asked.

Mr Jones passed over an enormous leather-bound book and Mr Hartwell examined it closely, slowly turning the pages. "Let's see . . . no, no that wouldn't do . . . mmm . . . there's a vacancy for a station lad at Hampton. How would that suit you?"

"Oh yes, please sir," said Robbie fervently.

"Good. Good. Mr Jones here will attend to all the details – medical examinations and so on. You do read and write I suppose?" he added as an afterthought, and Robbie's heart went into his mouth.

"I've been learning," he said cautiously.

"Have you now. Well, we'd better see how well you do. Here . . ." Mr Hartwell fumbled on the table and handed Robbie a sheet of paper . . . "read that to me."

Robbie took the paper with trembling hands. He looked down. The words were like strange black marks, shaking in his nervous hands. He began to panic, then he remembered Deborah saying to him, "Don't worry about *all* of it Robbie, just read the first word – the rest will follow." He looked at the first word and began to read: "Rules and Regulations for the Guidance of the Officers and Men." He read haltingly at first, then he grew more confident. "1. All persons employed by the Company must devote themselves exclusively to the Company's service; they must reside at whatever place may be appointed, attend at such hours as may be required, pay prompt obedience to all persons placed in authority over them, and conform to all the Rules and Regulations of the

Company. . . ." Robbie stopped reading and looked up. Mr Hartwell was smiling – a real smile this time.

"All right lad," he said, "you'll do."

Robbie gave a great sigh of relief.

"Any questions you would like to ask?" Mr Hartwell went on.

Robbie took a breath. "Well, yes sir. Please. You see – it's about my father. . . ."

The rest of the morning passed in a whirl. Robbie was conducted into another room and answered an enormous number of questions about himself. He then had a medical examination and answered even more questions. After that he was told he could go, and he left the impressive building and was in the pony and trap without quite realising how he had got there.

It was only much later, when he was driving home that Robbie began to think sensibly. He smiled to himself. He had not even asked the one question Mr Hartwell probably expected of him. He had no idea what a station lad was or did. They'd laugh at home when he told them, he thought, but he did not mind. He reached the crossroads and stopped. Should he go home to Tambour Cottage and tell Martha and Deborah the news or . . .? He turned the pony in the direction of the bridge where he knew John would be working.

Mr Fowler and Henry Bridgman were also at the bridge. They had been discussing some minor alterations when they had been waylaid by two reporters from a local newspaper.

"Mr Fowler, sir," called one of them. "May I tell our readers your feelings on seeing the work so near completion?"

Mr Fowler turned to him and thought for a moment. "A certain anxiety, and a certain satisfaction, gentlemen," he said finally.

"I understand that this bridge is the longest single-span cast-iron bridge in the world," said the other reporter. He referred to his notes: "One hundred and fifty feet isn't it, sir?"

"Two hundred feet," corrected Mr Fowler, "You must learn to be accurate, young man." The young reporter hurriedly changed his notes.

Mr Fowler continued rapidly. "We were fortunate to find a solid foundation of rock for the bridge, and on this basis an abutment of stone was erected on each side of the water." The reporters scribbled fast to keep up. "Stretching from abutment to abutment across the river are four iron girders, each of which is about four feet in depth, with a section of corresponding size. These bear the platform of the bridge. . . ."

Mr Bridgman coughed. They were already late for their next appointment. Mr Fowler waved him away. "One moment, Mr Bridgman, I must satisfy these gentlemen."

The gentlemen had caught up and were waiting, pens poised, for the next onslaught. Mr Fowler continued. "The imposts stand about twenty feet above the ordinary level of the water and the arch has a rise of about twenty feet more. On each side of the bridge there is a land arch of thirty feet across and the entire weight is about six hundred tons." He waited while the reporters caught up. "Is that sufficient for you, gentlemen?" he said.

"Yes, thank you, sir," replied one reporter, but the other asked: "Just one more thing, sir. Could you tell me, does the fact that this bridge is unique, being the first of its kind in the world, please you?"

Mr Fowler paused for a moment, then smiled slightly. "Of course," he said, "it is always gratifying to be first in any endeavour." He looked up at the bridge. It curved far above them, graceful and stark against the winter sky.

On the bridge, two gangs of navvies had been working non-stop for two days and two nights. John's butty was one of them and Robbie, who had left the pony and trap down by the river, climbed up the slope and carefully picked his way past the weary men until he reached his father.

"Pa – pa – I've got a job!" he called.

John straightened his back, and Robbie, who had not seen him for two days, was shocked. "Pa! You look done in," he said.

"It's a race laddie," John said wearily.

"I won't stay then," said Robbie and turned to go, but his father stopped him.

"Tell me about the job," he said.

"I'm to be station lad at Hampton," Robbie said proudly.

"That sounds grand."

"I don't know what I'm supposed to do though. I never asked," Robbie said ruefully. "Oh, I told them about you," he went on, "and they said there might be a job for you as ganger on the permanent way. You've to go and see them when the work here is done."

"That's good Robbie," said John warmly, "that's very good."

"Will you be home later?"

"If I can," John replied and closed his eyes for a moment. He opened them. "I must get on." He turned to the navvies. "Right lads. This section, then a break!"

Robbie stood for a moment watching the work, then made his way off the bridge and down the slope.

On the riverbank Mr Fowler was just finishing his press interview and was anxious to get away. Robbie passed close by Mr Fowler and heard the reporter say, "So to sum up Mr Fowler. . . ." The next thing he heard was a cry from the bridge, then a piercing scream followed by a loud splash.

For a split second there was a stunned silence. Then Mr Bridgman cried out: "My God, there's a man gone over!" and began to run up the slope. Mr Fowler and the reporters looked helplessly into the water as the ripples widened. A farmer's lad, herding some sheep along the track, dived headfirst into the river and another passerby went for a boat moored at the side.

Robbie had turned sharply at the first cry and stared at the bridge. The navvies had raced to the side and were lining the edge, craning their heads down to the water. Robbie's heart was pounding and he forced himself to look slowly, one by one, along the line of navvies . . . Spider, Baldy, Topper, Fat-Gut, Green-Eye, Lanky. . . .

"Pa," he said quietly. "Pa. . . ." Daddy Jones, Daddy Smith, Scarecrow, Yorky . . . his eyes filled and he could not see clearly any more. He raced up the slope to the bridge. "Pa! Pa!" he called. He reached the top and the navvies turned to face him. "Pa . . .?"

Green-Eye came forward and put his arm round his shoulders. "Come on lad," he said. "I'll take you home. He's gone."

14

Robbie was only dimly aware of being taken home. He felt he was living through some kind of nightmare where nothing was real, least of all the fact that his father was dead. He was vaguely aware of sitting in the parlour while Green-Eye told Martha and Deborah, but the only thing that remained with him afterwards was Martha's stricken face. He heard her say "You're sure it's him?" in a low, unsteady voice, and saw Green-Eye nod.

Some hours later two men came. They had recovered a body from the river and wanted someone to identify it. "A big fellow he was," they said cheerfully, "took four of us to get 'im out." He knew that Martha was looking at him but he couldn't move and he couldn't speak and she had said quietly, "I'll come." When she returned she had gone straight to her room and he had not seen her since.

Deborah had helped him up the stairs to the clean, white attic room, for he found he could not walk without help and he had stayed there, not eating, not sleeping, trying not to think. Every minute of every day he expected John to walk into the room, filling it with his large presence, and he could not weep because he could not believe that John was dead – it just wasn't possible.

Two nights later he went out and wandered round the village alone, expecting at every turning to see John striding towards him, smiling, asking him if he'd care for a jar before tea. The ferryman took him over the river and he went to the shanty. It was like a ghost town. Empty shacks, great piles of rubbish and a vast patch of mud-trampled earth was all that was left. He passed one or two men but no one stopped him and no one spoke to him. He sat on a rock for the remainder of the night and he knew then that John was dead and he thought that he could not bear it for the pain was worse, far, far worse than any he had endured with his foot. He went home at dawn and shut himself in his room.

And Martha? After Martha had identified the body she had gone straight to her room and stayed there.

Robbie and Martha next met at the funeral. It was a good funeral. Over two hundred navvies turned up from miles around, and it took six hefty men from John's own butty to carry the solid oak coffin. Martha, Robbie and Deborah walked silently behind it through the village streets.

Afterwards the navvies crowded round Robbie. "A good send-off wasn't it?" said Spider with morbid satisfaction, and Topper added, "I only hope I get as good a do at my funeral." Baldy said John would have been proud to have been part of it and Lanky asked Robbie what he was going to do now. Robbie turned and pushed his way past them out of the churchyard.

Mr Fowler and Henry Bridgman had also been at the funeral, although Robbie was unaware of them. He was also unaware that Mr Fowler himself had arranged for Robbie to be given compassionate leave – Robbie had forgotten completely about his new job.

That night the navvies celebrated the death in their own way. For the last time huge bonfires were lit at the shanty near Arley, and the navvies ended up roaring drunk. The following morning, those that were sober enough had gone, tramping off in search of new work.

Robbie spent the night in the alehouse. He sat alone in a corner, steadily drinking, trying to drink himself back into the numbness he had felt a few days ago. He listened to the navvies talk. There was work to be had in Scotland he heard, and he decided that that was where he would go. He drank on and on, but nothing would take away the pain or ease the desolate, lost feeling, and in the early hours of the morning he went back to Tambour Cottage.

The next day, the day on which the railway was to be opened, dawned fresh, clear and cold. Very early in the morning a group of villagers could be seen erecting bunting in the streets, and two men fixed a large banner right across from one side to the other which read: *Welcome to the Railway.*

The new station at Arley was also bedecked with bunting. Soon after dawn a man wearing an impressive uniform and top hat rode up on a bicycle. The new stationmaster of Arley wobbled to a stand, dismounted, took out a large bunch of keys, selected the right one and opened up the station. His staff arrived soon after and were to be seen hard at work with mops, brooms and buckets cleaning everything that could be cleaned.

There was also much cleaning taking place in the engine shed at Worcester Station. Two brand new locomotives – which had only arrived the previous night – were being cleaned, oiled and lovingly polished. The firemen, who had been up half the night, anxiously examined the fires they were building up in the boilers and the two drivers arrived hours before they were needed in order to make last-minute checks and prowl possessively round their engines.

The coach cleaners were also busy both on the insides and the outsides of the new coaches, and footwarmers and rugs emblazoned with the Company's crest were placed in the First Class compartments. All this was taking place while those who were to be the first occupants of the coaches were still snoring loudly in their beds.

At mile intervals along the entire track, lengthmen were walking, checking the track and sleepers and occasionally tapping a spike into place.

In the fields where the open-air feasts were to be held, great marquees had been erected and huge oxen were slowly roasting on spits while barrel after barrel of ale was unloaded from carts.

In the large hotel in Shrewsbury where the first of the celebratory dinners was to be held, mountains of food had already been prepared in the kitchens and the tables were being laid with snowy-white linen, gleaming silver and polished cut-glass. The Chef's masterpiece was ceremoniously wheeled in: a gigantic cake shaped to the Railway Company's crest and with the different colours picked out in marzipan and icing sugar. The Chef himself followed the trolley, hands clasped anxiously together, until the edifice was successfully mounted on the table.

Along the river bank a solitary figure on horseback was riding. It was still very early and the horse's hooves sounded sharp on the frosty ground. The man reached the foot of Victoria Bridge and looked up. John Fowler, later to design the great Forth Bridge in Scotland, and to become Sir John Fowler, stood and enjoyed a quiet moment alone with his bridge before all the bustle commenced.

The village of Arley had never had a morning like it before. Everyone was going to be there, somewhere along the track, to see the very first train pass. Even Amelia Gregory, eating her usual breakfast of weak tea and toast, thought that she *might* just happen to see what all the fuss was about –

if she was walking that way, of course.

The streets began filling up with people dressed in holiday finery and in holiday mood, all making their way down to the railway in order to secure the best vantage points. Children excitedly waved Union Jacks and a fair that had been opened in a nearby field by some enterprising gypsies did a roaring trade.

The Bewdley and Wyre Forest District Brass Band, which had the honour of accompanying the first train, arrived at Worcester Station and nervously polished their instruments, hoping they would remember the tune.

The first of the eminent guests arrived, anxious to get the best seats on the train. The Mayor and dignitaries of the local towns, the Board of Directors of the Company, the shareholders, local MPs and JPs, the Government's Board of Trade Inspector, the Chief Engineer and his staff, landed gentry of the area, local businessmen and traders, together with their respective wives and children, were guests of the Railway Company, invited to travel in the first train and partake of an impressive luncheon in Shrewsbury.

Mr Bridgman scurried from one end of the line to the other, shaking with nerves as he dealt with one crisis after another. His wife had arranged to bring his best suit to Worcester at eleven o'clock which would just give him time to wash and change in the gentlemen's lavatory before joining the rest of the assembled guests on the train, but he was worried that he would not be there in time.

Country folk from outlying farms miles away streamed into the towns and villages bordering the railway. Children with clean smocks and well-scrubbed hands and faces frightened each other with tales of the "iron monster" and everyone was in excellent spirits. Occasionally they passed navvies tramping away from the district, but little if any attention was paid to them.

By ten o'clock there were hundreds of people and a

general air of expectancy along the whole line, although the train was not due to leave Worcester until half past eleven.

In Tambour Cottage the blinds were drawn and the place seemed dead and lifeless. Up in his room Robbie was putting the finishing touches to packing his few belongings. He stopped and looked round the small room, then as a final gesture, he turned the row of dolls to face back into the room again. They stared at him unblinking and he stared back. Hastily he brushed his hand across his eyes, picked up his bundle, opened the door and went downstairs. At the bottom of the stairs he paused, looked at the closed door into the parlour and drew a deep breath. Then he went in.

It was very dim inside, for the curtains were still drawn. Martha was sitting in a chair by the unlit fire, a still, black figure. Deborah was at the table and got up when Robbie entered.

He stood awkwardly in the doorway. "Well – I'll be off," he said.

"Robbie . . ." Deborah moved to him and caught his arm. "Please don't go – please!"

"Don't, Debbie," he said, "it's hard enough as it is," and he turned to Martha. "I'll – I'll say goodbye. . . ."

Martha stared vacantly into the fireplace and made no move for a long moment. Then slowly she turned round. Her plain, round face looked as though it had been carved out of stone, and there were deep lines where there had been none before. She was not crying. She had done all her crying alone in her room and she had no tears left.

She looked blankly at Robbie and he was like a stranger. She felt there was nothing she could say to comfort him, for the pain went too deep.

Robbie bent his head and turned away, and the desolate look on his face moved her. She held out her arms. "You poor boy," she said and Robbie had dropped his bundle and was kneeling by her side, his head buried in her lap, sobbing as he had never been able to before.

"I can't stay here – I can't. It hurts too much. He was – he was – the best. . . ." Martha stroked his head gently. "Why did he have to die? I'm the worthless one – I'm the cripple – why wasn't it me? It's so – unfair. . . ."

"Ssh now," said Martha, "ssh."

Gradually Robbie's sobbing ceased. Martha lifted his head.

"Look at me," she said, "listen. God doesn't tell us why he takes one person and not another. We must just accept. But you – you shouldn't run away because of what's happened. You can't run away from your grief. It'll haunt you all your life if you do." She stopped.

"I can't stay and see trains run up and down over the spot where . . . I *can't*!"

Martha went on in a slow, halting voice: "He told me he'd left the Highlands when your mother died. He . . . he said he couldn't bear to stay anywhere for long. . . ." She paused. "Robbie, there's a home for you here and a job to go to . . ."

"I couldn't stay to see the railway thrive," said Robbie vehemently, "to work on it. Not after what it did to pa . . ."

"The railway will be here for a long, long time," said Martha, "perhaps for ever. Don't you think that's something to be proud of? That your father helped to build something as fine as that?"

Robbie was silent.

"Robbie, will you do something for me?" asked Martha. "Will you accompany Deborah and me to see the first train? And then, if you still want to go, I won't say another word."

Robbie slowly got up and Martha stood as well. She moved slowly as though she was stiff. "Deborah, fetch my shawl," she said, and leaned on Robbie as they went out of the room.

At half past eleven the first train left Worcester accompanied by cheers, flag-waving and the cheerful playing of the Bewdley and Wyre Forest District Brass Band. Detonators had been placed on the track and exploded loudly under the wheels of the engines.

Mr Fowler stood proudly on the footplate of the first locomotive along with Colonel Yolland from the Board of Trade and the Inspectors of the Severn Valley Railway and the West Midland Railway. The fireman and driver were finding it somewhat difficult to work with so many distinguished people on the small footplate.

Mr Bridgman had caught the train at the very last minute and was sitting exhaustedly in a First Class compartment trying to regain his breath. He closed his eyes for a second, and, to his lasting disgust, fell fast asleep.

The train reached Hartlebury, the start of the new Severn Valley line, and took on a third engine and fourteen more coaches. Among the guests of the railway to get on at Hartlebury were Mr Woodward of Arley with his wife and children.

An enormous crowd cheered the train in to Bewdley and the bells of St Anne's Parish Church vied with the brass band. More detonators added to the general noise and startled the new arrivals on the train, but did not disturb Mr Bridgman. He slept through everything.

The train slowed at the approach to Victoria Bridge. The bridge itself was decked with bunting and the river banks crammed tight with people. A small flotilla of boats waited with their occupants craning upwards to see the bridge.

Martha, Robbie and Deborah, three figures standing out in their black mourning clothes, made their way slowly through the crowds to the edge of the riverbank. They stood still, staring upwards, silent, busy with their own thoughts.

A spurt of excitement passed through the crowds as a distant whistle was heard. A small puff of smoke could be seen above the trees and a child began to cry. Distant cheering grew louder and louder and was taken up by everyone, long before the train appeared.

Another whistle, and the train could be heard and there it was, on the bridge. Passengers on the train waved down at the crowds and the crowds waved and cheered back. A man in one of the boats waved his hat so wildly that he overturned the boat and the party in it into the river, and the watchers on the banks cheered as they swam for shore.

The train crossed over the bridge and slowed down for the entry to Arley Station. The stationmaster and his staff stood stiffly to attention and the brass band once more broke into the well-known *Hail the Conquering Hero Comes* as the three engines and twenty-one coaches steamed gently into the crowded station and stopped.

After the train had gone from the bridge, Martha, Robbie and Deborah had stood silent for some time. Then, as the crowds round them streamed off to the station to look at the train, Robbie put an arm round each of them.

"Let's go home," he said.

The three of them turned and slowly walked away from the river and up the hill to Tambour Cottage.

FACT AND FICTION

The Severn Valley Railway Company was formed in 1852 to build a railway between Shrewsbury, the county town of Shropshire, and a junction at the village of Hartlebury in Worcestershire with the Oxford, Worcester and Wolverhampton Railway. The line follows the course of the River Severn, which until then had been the main transport route for the region.

Between 1858 and 1862, up to nine hundred railway navvies from all parts of the country were working on the construction. John Fowler was Consultant Engineer and Henry Bridgman was a site engineer.

Robbie and John Grant, Martha and Deborah, are all fictional characters and their story is also invented. But the dates, the background, and the technical information are as correct as historical research can make them. And I like to think that John Fowler, early on the morning of the line's opening, might have enjoyed a moment's quiet contemplation of his impressive Victoria Bridge. In 1862 it really was the longest single span cast iron bridge in the world.

In fact the Severn Valley line was never completely independent. It was leased to the West Midland Railway who operated the traffic on it from the moment it opened in 1862. The West Midland Railway was taken over by the Great Western Railway in 1863 and so the Severn Valley Railway became part of the G.W.R. – God's Wonderful Railway. When the railways were nationalised in 1948 the line became part of British Railways. It was closed, along with many other rural lines, in 1963.

But that was not the end of the story. In 1967 a group of enthusiasts formed a company to re-open the line as a privately-run preserved steam railway. It took the original name: The Severn Valley Railway. In 1980 it is still going strong.